TABLE OF CONTENTS

PREFACE

I wanted to start this off with the date of my Day 1, but I have no idea when that was.

I think I've always been entrepreneurial. I had lemonade stands, sold Girl Scout cookies, came up with ideas...but I was never the kid hustling in school. You know those stories: "this entrepreneur was buying bags of chips for .50 and selling them for $1 to kids in their high school." That wasn't me AT ALL (hello, anxiety).

I was a "One Day"-er in my teens and throughout college, thinking that it would be cool to have my own business as my main source of income, but I wouldn't *dare* to try.

And then I graduated and got hit with the cold, hard reality of the job marketplace. I came to realize very quickly that oh, a degree in Social Sciences *wasn't* going to put me in line for a 6 figure job right off the bat (or any job, sigh). I learned that a "traditional" career wasn't where I was comfortable, nor was it a path where I would find long term success.

After the Great Recession in the late aughts, many of us realized that we needed to work out multiple ways to support ourselves and our families, and I think this is especially true for Millennials and Gen Z'ers. We've had to learn, maybe a little cruelly, that the world is unkind and untenable to those who were sold the idea of job security, homeownership, and easy self-sufficiency.

What's truly bewildering is that many of us were branded as lazy when we struggled to find our place, or entitled when we wanted to have a little luxury to keep us going. Millennials helped to create the Hustle Culture movement, where we tried to show that it wasn't malaise, or apathy, or lack of work, but instead was an overdrive of working anywhere and everywhere we could just to get by. Those of us who didn't buy into that world or felt intimidated by it retreated inside our own worlds like a turtle in its shell, afraid to branch out and give it a go.

That's not to say I haven't tried to make it work the way I was "supposed to." I've been the head of Marketing Departments for a few companies, and while the money was nice, it always felt a little like I wasn't fitting into this world with its office politics and ego coddling.

Try as I might, the thought of doing the same job in the same office for the next 45 years gave me cold sweats. I spent months in therapy, trying to find a way to navigate this world and feel less depressed or overwhelmed by what I subconsciously knew was the wrong fit for me. I took pills to mitigate my anxiety and drank multiple glasses of wine every night to combat my emotions and prepare me for the next day. I spent a lot of money on things I didn't need so that I could justify why I was staying in the corporate world. None of it worked.

By the end, it was too late to pretend any of this was going to keep me complacent and numb to what I inherently knew was the wrong thing for me. I hated the slog so much that at my last "day job," I would drive in every morning asking the Universe to make them fire me because I was too afraid to let go of the money and benefits (the so-called "Golden Handcuffs"). Thankfully during a bitterly cold day in March, my wish was granted, and I was brought into an office and told I was being let go.

I tell you that if it hadn't been icy out, I would've skipped out of the building all the way to my car, I was **so** happy. Just one week later, I sat down in First Class on a plane heading towards California and my very first speaking gig.

While I tried to fight it, I knew where I was meant to be early on even though, maybe like you, I tried to find ways to be a traditional employee. However, I've gained enough experience to understand that my life, for better or worse, is meant to be carved out of my own making. At times it can be difficult and painful but now my fate is in my control and mine alone.

Thanks to this insatiable drive inside of me, I've seen my name in the New York Times. I've won 5 awards for one of my businesses, beating out ginormous conglomerates. I've paid for our house, cars, and vacations in full with cash. I've spoken at conferences where I was touted as a "Marketing Expert" and had the opportunity to coach entrepreneurs who want to connect with their customers but aren't sure how.

I can say fully that I am living my dream life and that I want the same for you. I want you to stop being afraid of the "what ifs," to stop talking yourself out of following your dreams, and to create the plan that moves you closer to where you *know* you're supposed to be.

This book contains the steps I followed, sometimes as lessons learned the hard way, in order to evolve into the entrepreneur who got to carve out her own path. This book also includes supplemental guides to reference when your business life stumbles a little, as all of ours do once in a while, and the steps you can take to ride it out.

What this book *doesn't* include, though, is a lot of filler. The goal of **Day 1** isn't to overwhelm you with information that will get in the way of your progress; I want this to be your roadmap to success, so I've left out a lot of the "scenic rest stops" if you will.

Lastly, I wanted this book to be less of a feel-good fluff piece, and more of an actionable guide so that you know exactly (or, pretty close to exact) the steps you're going to have to take to get your business launched. Of course, some nuances will be relevant to only your niche, so you might need to give things a little "*some restrictions may apply,*" but I've tried to cover as much as possible so that you have the right tools to get going.

How to Use This Book

There is no "behind" on Day 1, so take your time to implement the steps laid out here before opening your business. I know that you're ready to hit the ground running (I'm the same way), but you got this book because you wanted to do it the right way, so let's actually do that! Go through the chapters in order, completing the steps you need to move your business forward, and remember that you're no one else's timeline but your own!

If you want to be a superstar pupil, I'd recommend reading through the book in its entirety (again, I've cleared out a lot of the static noise and made this a lean guide to getting you to where you want to be), then go back and reread each chapter at a time, digesting the information and implementing the tools to ramp up your path to success.

We're in all of this together, and we need what you're about to create, so let's get going to make this world a better place!

INTRO - SO YOU WANT TO BE AN ENTREPRENEUR?

First off, very cool. Welcome to a world of infinite possibilities.

Before I go off sounding even more like Willy Wonka or like I've been sitting in the Lotus Position on a mountain for the past decade, let's talk about what it means to be an entrepreneur. (And no, we're not starting this off with Webster's Dictionary definition.)

Entrepreneurship means an opportunity to be:

Creative - a chance to put your hands into the clay and create something from nothing.

Free - free from office politics, glass ceilings, crushing burn out.

Responsible - the buck stops with you through the good times...and especially the bad.

Emotional - some moments will take your breath away, moments when you'll cry from joy or defeat, times when you'll have to push your feelings down for the greater good, and times when you'll never be able to look back at the person you used to be.

Vulnerable - you'll put yourself out there, release this baby into the world and become immediately open to the love and/or criticism of a huge world of customers and chances.

Amazed - Every email, every 5-star review, every genuine testimonial will astound you and give you a sense of awe at the effect your business has had on others.

Terrified - Bills will come that will keep you awake at night, confusing regulations might pop up in your industry that seem to come from nowhere, another pandemic could wipe your income off the map.

Alone - Owning your own business is a lonely road for those who are used to being in an office environment. There will be days when you're desperate for some camaraderie that your laptop simply can't give, or moments when you'll feel that no one else in the world could understand what you're going through.

Unencumbered - The rules are yours to write and rewrite as you see fit.

So yes, it's a mixed bag but really, aren't all things? You deciding to pick up this book and take action means that you're ready to take this on, this passion of yours, and while I might not know you personally, I *do* know that makes you a certain type of person who sees a list like that and says "bring it on."

Before I set you off into the world of entrepreneurship, let me give you a shortcut past those who are just fumbling around and dive into what I think are the 3 key factors to being a successful entrepreneur that you should cultivate:

1. **An ability to be proactive** - This is especially hard for introverts, and I sympathize. It's not easy to put yourself out there and be vulnerable as you offer a product or service that was created by you, but to be an entrepreneur means you'll have to be a rainmaker and not wait for the rain to come. You'll have to step out of the comfort bubble and ask for the sale or the press mention. You won't be able to wait for things to happen.

2. **An understanding of priorities** - Your life will be a perpetual balancing act as you navigate growing a business and maintaining a personal life. There will be times when your family priorities pull against the push of your business needs and vice versa, and you will have to assess which priority is the most pressing at that time. It's not impossible to have it all in a general way, but it is impossible to have it all at the exact same time. You'll have to be confident in your ability to understand the needs of your life and balance them against the pulls of your wants.

3. **A confidence in the self** - That's a pretty zen sorta way to say something, isn't it? "A confidence in the self" is my flourished way of saying: you're going to have to be secure enough in your choices, actions, and all-around self to be able to ask for help. It's a fool's errand to try to do this all on your own and carve a path in the mountain when there's already a 4 lane highway 50 feet to the left that someone else already built. Being stubborn, closed off, and suspicious gets you nowhere fast, so take it upon yourself to be open to reaching out to peers, competitors, gurus, whomever, and asking for their guidance.

Master those 3 things and baby, you're on your way to making snow angels in piles of dollar bills.

So now, let's go get you ready for your first day as an entrepreneur!

Ready? (duh)

Let's begin.

CHAPTER 1: HANDLING OBJECTIONS

Beginning your own business can be a terrifying prospect in some ways. You're building this thing with the hopes that it will prosper enough to support you and your goals, and some of those goals might include other people. There aren't any guarantees that it will work no matter how much you plan or how hard you work...sometimes the difference between being successful in business comes down to just dumb, stupid, infuriating *luck.

*(Side note: as I was writing this, my autosuggest switched out "luck" for "people." Oh, Apple, you know my heart.)

Well-intentioned (whether genuine or not) people will come at you from all directions with "thoughts," "concerns," or "suggestions" when it comes to launching your business. Unfortunately, it's just an inevitability that you'll need to be prepared to handle. Even more unfortunate is that they won't stop coming to no matter the level of success you have as an entrepreneur. It becomes as routine and cumbersome as your quarterly taxes.

So how do you navigate a path to success when those other people are blocking your way?

I've been incredibly fortunate that my husband has never doubted my drive to succeed. Any crazy idea or plan I've had for a business plan has never had to go through a gauntlet of negativity with him - quite the opposite. He's been my "Ride or Die" throughout.

That's not to say, though, that he hasn't had questions or been, let's say, *slightly* concerned when the rent was due, but through it all, he is a great support system.

I've been through the flip side of this, too, and I know there are times you might feel like you're in a hostile environment with no support, so let's talk about how you can handle it and push your way through.

Objections will come at you from all sides when you're starting something new. They're often cloaked as coming with "good intentions," but they can undermine you breathtakingly fast if you let them. The key to getting through them has a good defense, so let's tackle that.

How to Handle Outside Objections

To me, outside objections are the least of my worries as an entrepreneur, and one that you should accept as par for the course when creating your new business. But that doesn't mean you should lie down and accept your fate, no! Your job is to get ready for these objections and face them with a solid plan.

So what goes into your plan? The trick to overcoming objections is two-fold:

- A strong conviction
- A mature defense

A Strong Conviction

The first time I saw my name and my company in the New York Times was surreal. It felt truly vindicating, and like I was able to prove to myself and others that I was on the right path.

When a distant family member with whom I hadn't seen in decades found out through the family grapevine, I was told their immediate reaction was "Huh. Do you know what she should do? [Insert mediocre advice that I don't remember here]"

I just rolled my eyes when I heard this secondhand. I couldn't even have a moment of pride accomplishing this, really? Suddenly everyone had advice!

This, my love, will happen with you, as well. No matter the ups, people will expect you (with some hurtful levels of certainty) to have downs. They will feel obligated to let you know how you're screwing it up and how they are somehow more qualified than you to understand your situation.

What should you do?

Evaluate their credibility. There is nothing else to do here. If they are someone with whom you have a level of respect for then consider the point they're trying to make. Maybe there is some sage wisdom being shared here that you should unpack. Ask more questions and come from a place of curiosity to understand.

If, however, they have no credibility whatsoever and are not directly affected by your income, disregard their opinions, and keep going.

Having a strong conviction in your ability to achieve your goals can be the seal that prevents these "suggestions" from putting cracks in your foundation. Understand that many times you'll be the target of other people's insecurities because they're afraid to take the risk, and they'll project onto you some truly disturbing heaps of fears.

Your job is not to internalize their problems. Your job is to run your business.

A Mature Defense

That's not to say, though, that you should be bull-headed or throw a tantrum when some tough questions get asked. There are going to be times when you'll feel attacked by someone who is asking objectively good questions that you're not interested in facing.

Some of that is internal, and we'll get into that later in this chapter, but for the moment, let's talk about how to handle tough questions from people in your life who have earned the right to get an answer.

Let's say the question is about your experience. You want to begin a career as a life coach to leave your job as a corporate accountant. To someone who doesn't witness your inner thought process, this might seem like a jump. Why life coaching? What makes you qualified to handle someone else's life? You've been a number cruncher for a Fortune 500 company, so where is the life coaching advice coming from?

Or let's tackle another big topic you'll inevitably have to address: money. How are you going to pay your bills? What is this business going to cost to start? Where is that money coming from? Why are you going to charge so much/so little?

To a new entrepreneur, these are incredibly difficult and emotional questions to answer. You want to believe you'll succeed, and you're working hard to keep a positive mindset, so if everyone could just back off, that would be great.

Alas, we have to be adults and interact with the rest of the world, so rather than hiding from these questions, let's address them:

How to Handle Tough Questions

1. **Prepare ahead of time**. Even your most supportive friends and family will be curious about your decisions, so set yourself up ahead of time to receive these questions. To do this requires two big steps of work: not getting defensive and answering these questions for yourself.

   Not getting defensive: If these people are close to you, then accept their question as genuine curiosity and concern for you as a loved one. Most of the time, it's not a personal attack but an honest question that popped into their heads. Be thankful for the level of caring they have for you, an answer from a place of love and not hurt.

   Answer these questions for yourself: Part of being an entrepreneur is taking decisive action through steps towards a goal, and the questions above (How are you going to pay your bills? And so on..) are valid questions that you'll need to answer ahead of time anyhow. I think traditional business plans have gone the way of the VCR thanks to the ability to start a business online quickly, but that's not to say there isn't invaluable information that comes from sitting down and writing out a detailed plan of what you want to accomplish, how you'll do it, and why you'll be able to do what your competitors seemingly can't. Please take the time to at least journal out your answers to this and keep them nearby.

2. **Features v. Benefits**. If you've ever been a part of my Stop Sucking at Marketing class, then you're an expert on this and know what to do here. If you haven't signed up for it, let me give you a quick rundown: fea-

tures tell, benefits sell. When answering tough questions about your qualifications, answer it with a focus on how your experience will solve someone else's problems, not your own. For the former-Accountant-turned-Life-Coach, you could use your experience navigating the corporate world and seeing how mastery of X life skill has had a track record of proven success in your own life, and in the life of your colleagues so now it's your duty to utilize this knowledge to help others who are struggling to get to the next level in their lives. Helping them master X skill will give Y result....so on and so forth.

Do you see how the answer was framed? It wasn't, "Because I want to change my career and try something new." Instead, the answer was about your client and the solution they'll achieve working with you. You focused on them and not you. That's the benefit of your role as a Life Coach.

3. **Give them just enough info.** I'm all-too guilty of going into a monologue about my business when someone asks a tough question. In the end, it just confuses the person and makes me feel like I'm trying to justify my actions. Now I try to get straight to the root of the question, answer it, and then shut up. If they want more information, then the process repeats, but I make a conscious effort not to go further than the question.

That's not to say that everyone gets one-word responses, far from it! Rather, I suggest trying to answer like it was a short answer question on a test. Come at the question directly, and don't try to circumnavigate it by rambling on. "How will you earn an income?" "Through A, B,

C, and D."

4. **Move on.** Don't hold someone else's curiosity against them. If you feel attacked, either remove yourself from the conversation or change the subject. If you truly feel they weren't malicious, but you're still a little miffed, I'd recommend doing the same thing: change the subject or excuse yourself for some reason and take a minute to recoup. The point is that this moment doesn't need to affect you in the long run, so don't let it.

Handling Internal Objections

Imposter Syndrome is nefarious as fluff (trying to keep it PG here, but I'm sure you can replace "fluff" with your preferred four-letter word).

If you're unfamiliar, Imposter Syndrome (IS) is the internal struggle most, if not all, people have when it comes to their place in the world. It's a feeling that there are others out there who are better at doing what you do, and it spans all things: fitness, business, relationships, money, etc. It's especially prevalent in the entrepreneurial world, and very few are immune to it.

IS can start the minute you think of a new business idea. It's the "Yeah, but..." that rarely goes away, no matter how long you're in business.

When I first thought about writing this book, my IS was right there to block me. "What right do I have to write this book? Who would want to listen to what I have to say? Clearly, I should leave this to the pros who do this for a living."

But you know what? I *am* doing this for a living; I *am* one of the pros. I've been writing about entrepreneurship and marketing for nearly a decade and yet I still get feelings like I'm unqualified as compared to others.

IS can deflate an idea before it's even fully founded if you let it. So let's develop a set of tools to stop it from making you give up on your dreams.

For the exercise below, I'll use my own argument I had with myself writing this book so you can see how to work through it.

How to Break Away from Imposter Syndrome

1. **Confront it**. Yes, there are hundreds of really qualified people who can tell you how to start your business. This fact is true. What's also true is that I have a unique voice, and my experience is vastly different than anyone else's, so I can give a perspective that might relate to someone that couldn't get on board with another coach.

2. **Answer the question**. I have the right to write this book because it's inside of me; I am compelled to be this person who helps others achieve their business goals. My target demographic (the Avatar work I've done) wants to hear what I have to say because I am speaking to **them**.

3. **Acknowledge the lesson behind it.** I'm afraid that no one will read my book, or that someone will read it and find that it wasn't helpful. I'm afraid to let someone down, and that's why I'm feeling like I'm an inadequate person to give you this advice.

4. **Talk it out.** I really want to write this, but I keep feeling blocked by this sense that I'm not the right fit for the job so I'm going to speak with my therapist about why I feel this way and I'm going to set up a call with my business coach and work out the steps I need to make my book happen, regardless of the insecurities I'm feeling.

Objections will continue to come at you throughout the lifespan of your business; it's just a fact of entrepreneurship. But rather than shying away from the confrontation of uncomfortable questions (both from others and from your inner voice), learn the ways you can answer the questions and leverage them to your advantage. I believe in you to do it!

CHAPTER 2: DON'T BUILD SOMEONE ELSE'S EMPIRE

So let's talk a little about Influencers...and why those Tummy Teas are the worst.

Caveat: I have never had one of those teas, and I know they're not really a thing anymore, but you remember them, right? Teas which promised flat stomachs and, I don't know, millions of dollars and boyfriends? I'm sounding flippant about them, I know, and hey...maybe they really did work.

But here's why I have no idea about the validity of their claims (though I can take a guess): because I got so GD sick of seeing them everywhere on Instagram that I went scorched earth and unfollowed anyone who was posing with a stupid tea. Fitness Influencers, Lifestyle Influencers, freaking Pet-Based Influencers were hocking them! It was relentless.

I've been trying to find some statistical data to back up my hypothesis, but since statisticians aren't really concerned about Instagram and the ratio of unfollows based on an unoriginal shilling of products, I'll have to use my ~Marketing Specialist~ experience to say: that was the dumbest marketing idea for Influencers, which most likely hurt them (albeit rarely permanently), but somewhat brilliant for the Tea people.

Brilliant for the Tea people because their message got slammed out to millions of people. The same message, the same talking points, the nearly identical poses. Their brand marketing was top notch.

Dumb for the Influencers because it wasn't hard to see that they were all doing the same thing, and no one was standing out.

"But Megan," you say, "clearly those Influencers are successful because they got paid to hock those teas!" To which I say, "Yes, hopefully, they were paid directly because if it were affiliate sales instead, they just gave it all up for no guarantee."

What I mean by that is: by signing up to promote a product where (and again, speculating here but based on context clues, I'm pretty sure I'm right) the talking points were given, the imagery and product position were...let's say "heavily suggested," and the majority of what made the Influencers unique was lost. Which means what made people follow them was also lost. Which means they sold their Unique Selling Proposition (USP) for some gross tea.

If they didn't get paid until they brought in sales, then there wasn't anything to differentiate Follower1 from using Influencer1's affiliate link or Influencer2's link. Or Influencer36's link. Because it was all the same, so yes, I hope they got paid out directly instead.

Which (finally!) brings me to the point of this chapter: If you want to succeed in a long term kind of way, you're going to have to build your own business. LulaRoe consultants are filing class action lawsuits against the company, Shakeology shakes are gross, Amway bankrupts families on a weekly basis. Hitching your wagon to someone else's star means that you're beholden to their rules, their payment structures, and their whims.

Your job as an entrepreneur is to take care of yourself, your customers, and your credit card bills. As long as you're able to act ethically, there's a ton of flexibility in there to run a business on how you want to run it and create products that move you. Is it easier to sell Mary Kay lipsticks instead of your own line of vegan, organic lip creams? Not really.

With the lip creams, you're able to talk about the colors, the ingredients, the packaging, and why it moves you, why you're so passionate about it. Why you felt compelled to get these out into the world, you'll most likely start to get self-conscious because you won't shut up about them, and that's the awesome part (not the self-consciousness...sing the praises of your lip creams to anyone that doesn't run away!)

You know why? One of the secrets that the top salespeople of the world will tell you is that customers aren't usually buying a product, they're buying an experience, *and that's why*. What's even truer, especially with small businesses, is that customers aren't buying a product, they're buying into a person.

They see your giddy monologue about lip creams, and they want to feel that way, too. Or they want to look at that painting you made on their walls and talk to their guests about how the artist spoke for 15 minutes about why they chose that shade of red. Or they like how much you swear on your podcast because it shows your genuine emotions, so they want you to be their Marketing Coach (true story!). The customer wants to hold on to something intangible and put it away in their memory banks. That's what they're buying, not the plastic tube with the label and the wax and oils that were poured into it.

Maybe in the beginning it feels easier just to pay some sign-up fee and become an essential oil consultant. Look, I get it. It's hard to create a product, put it out into the world, and say, "This is mine. This is from me. I want you to validate it by giving me money for it so that you can have part of me with you." But if you want to be in this for the long term, you're going to have to birth that business baby and put it all over Facebook.

Remember that you're starting Day 1 to be free from an overbearing boss, or back-stabbing office culture, or policies which seem obtuse and outdated, so why would you jump right back into that because they promised you could be a "boss babe" if you simply pay this $5,000 start-up fee? Take that $5k and put it towards your own creativity and be the REAL Boss Babe you were meant to be.

CHAPTER 3: ESTABLISHING YOUR PLAN

Before we get started in this chapter, I just wanted to tell you that I'm **so** glad you're here. It's a big step to take, finally deciding to get up and get your business going. So many people have those "wouldn't it be cool if..." or "I'd really love to..." and never make it happen. But you're not one of those people. You're ready, you're able, and you're ready to get started, so let's get to it.

Let's get to it...by working backward. Ugh, this officially turned into homework, didn't it?

Keeping It Real...ly in Perspective

The first step is to develop an attainable goal and maintain realistic expectations. Obviously, **I** think you're going to be incredibly successful, but overnight successes are either few and far between, or misleading marketing and not something you should use as a benchmark or proof of your concept.

Sustaining Success in business means a long grind, but I don't say that to scare you away (don't close this book just yet!) instead to let you know it's okay to stumble along the way. No one has this figured out on Day 1, but we're still miles ahead of One Dayers.

Now, to sound a little contradictory (the curse of the Libras), that doesn't mean you shouldn't dream big. When I say "realistic," I mean a well thought-out plan and not just an "I'm going to be an Instagram influencer and make bank traveling the world!" That's not a plan or a goal, just a daydream.

What it really means to "dream big" to me at least, means what amounts to an essay (so yes, homework. Sorry, guys.) that explains a goal with measurable actions and realistic timeframes. To do that, you need to think SMART (more on that in a sec).

Start with your vision of a successful business. Here are some questions to get you started, though there are many more, so don't feel like you have to answer just these. Go big with it and draft out as much as you want:

- What does your business look like?
- Are you in a dedicated office space with a staff, or are you a traveling digital nomad who picks up work between flights to exotic locations?
- How much money is in your bank account?
- What assets do you own, and what assets does your business own?
- What sort of retirement savings do you have?
- Are you paying employees or independent contractors?
- How involved are you with the day-to-day?
- What does your fan base look like?
- Are you in Vogue, Town & Country, and hundreds of publications, or is your business more of a cult favorite?
- Will your products be sold in stores, will you focus solely on e-commerce, will you be solely service-based, or will it be a hybrid of all?
- What does your product line look like?
- Are you seen as a guru in your industry, or do you shy away from media attention?
- Do you travel for your business? Where to and why?

- Do you attend conferences and book speaking gigs?
- Is your family involved? Does your partner work outside the business, or do you solely support the family? Do you envision your kids or grandkids working in the family business?
- Will you sell the business when you're ready to retire, give it to your employees, or just close it down? (Exit goals are always important, so don't skip those!)

Okay, whew, that's a whole lotta questions; we just dove right in, didn't we? Now that you've brainstormed your ideal business goals let's work out how to get there.

In marketing, there's a term called "SMART goals" and it's an acronym for working out the mechanics of how a goal can be achieved. It usually involves critical thinking and some hard talks with yourself about aspects of a goal. Essentially, SMART methodology breaks down a goal into ways it can *actually* be achieved.

Now that you have your "business goal stream of consciousness," let's make it SMART.

How to Determine if Your Goal is SMART

Is your goal:
Specific?
This is what we worked out with all of those questions. Your goal can't be "I want to be famous!" but instead "I want to become an industry darling of [niche] [and what "famous" means in that field goes here]"

Measurable?
An effective goal has a specific benchmark to it: can it be definitively crossed off a list when it's achieved? What does "success" actually mean in concrete, black and white metrics? This is usually where we start to work out milestones (more on that

later).

Actionable?

"Famous AF!" isn't actionable. What are the steps that go into being a rockstar entrepreneur? This is the meat of milestones.

Realistic?

Losing 40lbs in 2 weeks isn't realistic unless you're cutting off limbs. The same goes for business goals. A million in net revenue on a bootstrapped business within the first four months? It's not *completely* unrealistic, but Realistic relies heavily on Measurable and Actionable to be vetted. Take a hard look at your goal and be honest about the amount of work that will go into achieving it.

Timed?

This always feels like the least fair part to me, but having a set schedule with a deadline helps to keep you focused on achieving what your goals are. Remember to be kind, but aggressive when it comes to setting a timeline. Push yourself, but not so much that you're having a breakdown on Month 3 because you left your day job and haven't replaced that income with your side business.

Setting Milestones

An unavoidable part of SMART goals is the establishment of milestones to help with the "cross off-ability" of your dreams. If you've ever dieted or tried to lose weight, you probably know that it's better to focus on the small wins rather than the final amount of weight you want to lose.

Keeping your head down and grinding towards that next 5lb loss is what most fitness gurus recommend, and the same goes for business.

A milestone is simply a 5lb chunk (I know, poor choice of

words in a weight-loss analogy) in a 100lb goal. It's a way to ensure you're going on the right path and will help move you forward towards your goals.

As an aside, one thing that I don't see a lot of discussions about with other business folks is how milestones can also show if you're on a path that needs to change. We set milestones at the beginning of a project that sometimes never come to fruition, so we need to evaluate if it's the right milestone to strive for, or if it's instead a sign that there is a better way to do something.

Here's an example: My first business, Metropolis Soap Co., had a "pulp horror" aesthetic. Soaps were named things like "The Black Soap Horror" and "Sea Mud...of Death!" with kitschy pulp comic women. My goal was to have the business support me, pay off my student loans, and I was going to accomplish that by working the craft show circuit and getting my skincare and soap into Whole Foods.

Little did I realize that "pulp horror" skincare wasn't really the kind of product Whole Foods buyers and customers were interested in so I came to a wall before hitting that milestone. If I wanted to keep going down that path, I would have to adapt my business or pick a different route.

In the end, I updated the branding to be more "natural" and crunchy, which created interest in the brand way more when I went to wholesale trade shows like the Natural Products Expo.

For the record, not only did my branding change, but I also ended up changing my path and dropped the idea of getting into Whole Foods because of their pricing demands and requests (they're a big fish and can push that weight around onto smaller manufacturers, and it just wouldn't have supported my end goal).

Milestones can be as large or as small as you want. You can have 10 milestones or 500, and it's really dependent on what motivates you more. I usually recommend starting with 3 - 5 for one specific part of your goal.

Let's say you want to focus on building your brand as your goal for this year (which you've broken down from your larger goal of world domination, of course). The end result of working on your brand is that you'll have a specific branding guide so that you have a full set of logos, colors, fonts, and a distinct look (think about Tiffany's and their signature shade of blue). What milestones would you set that would help you reach this goal?

If it were me, I would say:

I will develop my ideal customer profile in 4 weeks

I will pick a logo that would attract that customer to my brand in 6 weeks
  1. Research options for logos
  2. Hire a designer or design it myself
  3. Get variations of the logo that include different sizes, grayscale, etc

I will pick a color palette that is complementary to my products in 1 week
  1. Research competition to see what colors are used: is there a common hue? Do I want to emulate that or stand out?
  2. I will pick a main color, 2 complementary colors, and 1 contrasting color for emphasis and accents

I will set standards for fonts in 1 week
  1. Research fonts and the rights for each font
  2. Pick sizes and specifics (can you use italics, bold, etc.)
  3. Make sure fonts will work across multiple platforms (website, print, etc)

Right there is 12 weeks of milestones towards my end goal of a consistent branding strategy. If I knocked that out in 12 consecutive weeks, I'd have a quarter of the year down, and 3 more quarters to test out the brand and make changes, or I could consider the goal achieved and move on!

SWOT Analysis

If you're ready to put your big marketing pants on and try your hand at some high-level work, then you're going to love creating your SWOT Analysis.

That said, this is a dense topic that will require some hard research on your end, but let me try to get you through it as best as I can.

In all actuality, you can skip this if you really want, though you're only hurting yourself by not doing it. Also, I won't be mad, just disappointed. (Mom always knew how to guilt me into doing stuff!)

SWOT stands for Strengths, Weaknesses, Opportunities, and Threats, and is quintessential for any business owner to understand. It's usually drawn out as a grid similar to this:

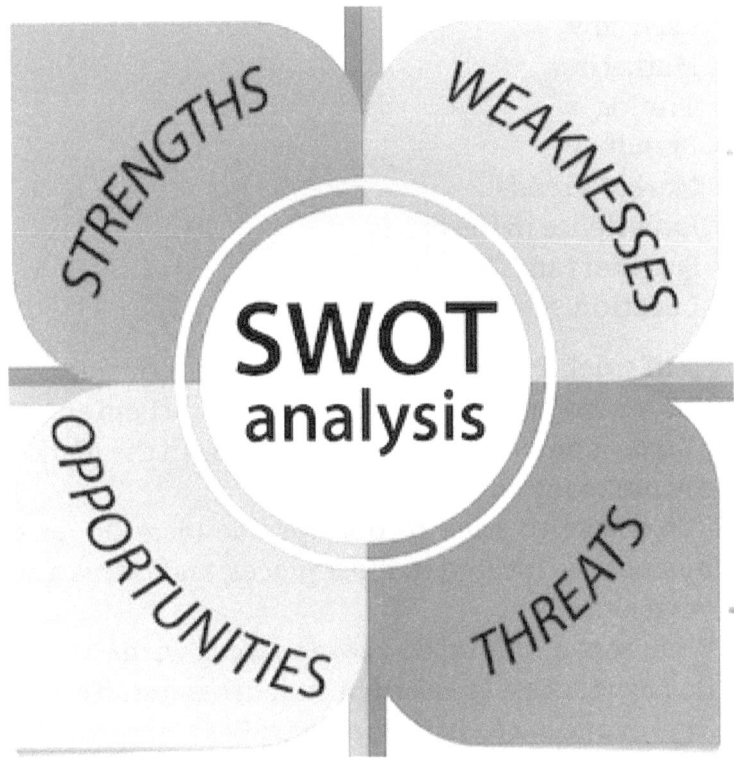

Learning how to analyze these 4 points of a business is crucial, as it will give you an understanding of your marketplace and how you can find a niche to conquer.

Strengths and Weaknesses relate to internal business matters. Things like cash flow, experience in the industry, strong branding, a great network to help you get the word out, things like that. What do you think you'll be good at as a business owner, and where will you need help?

Opportunities and Threats apply to external forces. What are your competitors in the field doing, how saturated is your marketplace, and what opportunities are out there for you to make an opening with and take the world by storm?

Some examples of things to consider in a SWOT analysis (it's your call where they should go!)

- Cash flow
- Marketing
- Timing
- Branding
- Market Trends
- Experience in the industry
- Suppliers and Vendors
- Location

If you're still stuck, here are some questions to consider:

- Who are my competitors, and what sets them apart?
- Do my competitors miss something in the market that I can use to my advantage?
- Do I have to stick to one specific location, or can my business be located in most places, and is this a strength or weakness?
- What sort of capital do I have to work with?
- Do I have access to the right support and staff?
- Am I experienced in this industry?
- What are the current market trends like?
- Is there an opportune time of year for me to open my business?
- What technology do I have available to me to help run the business, and what tech will I need to get?
- Is my target market growing or shrinking?
- Do I have a network of contacts I can utilize to help me get the word out?
- Are there regulations in your industry that are prone to change as you grow?
- Do you have access to suppliers and vendors?
- Do you have backups and Plan Bs in effect in case your vendors or suppliers are no longer reliable?

Developing an Avatar

The last part for us to cover is to develop your ideal customer. I know that in the beginning, you'll take anyone's money who's willing to pay, but if you're ready to build a successful, long-term business, you're going to need to cut down your pool of potential customers.

This sounds counterintuitive, I know! Think about it like this:

You want to create a social media advertising campaign to promote your upcoming product launch. You have a budget of $500 and want to use it across Instagram and Pinterest over the period of a month to ramp up the launch.

You start going through the Pinterest and Instagram targeting options but don't really know who you want to target, so you keep it pretty broad, hoping that you'll hit a variety of people who would be interested in your product. So you say you want to target women, ages 18 - 64, who live in the United States.

At the time of this writing, Facebook (which owns Instagram) says that would be 120,000,000 people, not even counting Pinterest users. While that sounds amazing, that doesn't mean that 120,000,000+ are actually looking at your ad or are interested in your product. The sad reality is that your $500 budget would be shot in less than a few days and have a low chance of hitting the person who would love your product the most.

Version 2 of this is that you've started with women, ages 18 - 64, who live in the United States but drilled it down a little.

Let's say your product is a new clothing line that has a retro vibe to it. Well, you don't want to target people who hate the vintage look, that would just waste your budget. So you start to look for potential customers who would be into things like Bettie Page, pin up girls, 1950's beauty, finger waves, and things like that. Your product line is going to be a little more on the high end in terms of pricing, so you add interests like vintage Chanel, antique shopping, etc.

After that, you start to think that your age bracket is a little too wide, so you chunk that down to women in their 30s - 50's, as they would have a better shot at having the income that would afford them the ability to invest in clothing like yours. If they have a higher-than-average income, it's not unreasonable to think that they also have a college degree, so you add that as a requirement for your targeting (the sad reality of all the things Facebook knows about you).

Now you've significantly cut your potential audience, but you've done so in such a way that you now have a more dedicated niche of buyers who would be way more interested in your clothes. Now that $500 budget can go to showing a smaller pool of people your ad multiple times instead of a one-off shot, which makes them begin to notice you and your message (most people mentally block out ads and need to see it at least 5 times before paying attention). You're upping your shot at converting by hitting these ideal customers up multiple times, do you see the difference?

This is the baseline of an avatar, which is just a term that means your ideal customer. It will feel cheesy, and sometimes make you uncomfortable to think about as it means excluding categories of people, but helps you create a laser focus and lower your outreach time and costs. I talk more about this in my Stop Sucking at Marketing course, but here are some ways to get started:

Things to Consider When Creating an Avatar

- Gender
- Age range
- Education

- Income
- Likes
- Dislikes
- Hopes
- Fears
- Marital Status
- Family (kids?)
- Location
- Job
- Aspirations

Once you flesh out your avatar, lean into the cheesy-ness of it and give it a name like you would if you just birthed a new human baby. I know how bizarre that sounds, but by creating a new imaginary frien....er...avatar, you're able to envision an actual person better, and this can help you in the long run when you work on branding, social media, advertising, and even product lines.

CHAPTER 4: DO THE SCARY STUFF AND VALIDATE YOUR IDEA

So you've got this amazing idea, and you absolutely know it's going to be the thing that catapults you into billions of dollars and can finally let you tell your boss to kiss it.

Awesome. But how do you really know?

Here's the answer, which sounds so simple you'll wonder why the hell you're bothering to read this:

You test it.

Now here's the scary part: You test it by asking for money, from strangers.

Here's the thing: your family and best friends are *totally* into your idea and will *definitely* help you share your posts on Facebook to promote it, but when it comes to launching your business for orders, all of that support doesn't mean a thing when it's time to pay the bills.

To ensure that your product or service is actually viable and will help get you to where you want to be, you need to test it on the marketplace and see quantifiable results.

Support and likes on Instagram are great, but there's a difference between "knowing" what people want and actually finding out what it is that convinces them to open their wallets.

Back when I was making soap and candles, I "knew" the products that my customers would want and go crazy for, so I would create dozens of products and wait for the cash to roll in.

Except I never actually asked my customers what they wanted, so I was spending hundreds to thousands of dollars throwing darts and hoping I'd land on the right thing. Instead, I'd be stuck with 17 soaps, 10 scrubs, a face care line no one asked for, and countless other products that "seemed" great, but never converted into money.

In my opinion, and for the people who got the products for free when I needed to clear the inventory, they were great products...but because I wasn't willing to test them first, they ended up as a loss because I was too afraid to ask for commitments up-front. It felt impolite to ask my customers to stand behind me with their funds with the promise of a not-yet-launched product.

Here's the thing: today this is not as scary as it used to be. Pre-sales through sites like Kickstarter or GoFundMe help validate an idea before production begins. For services, taking early adopters on through pre-registration offers can test how well your positioning is for a potential customer base.

Today it's way easier to validate an idea with moolah than it used to be, and can give you a little bit of a buffer between asking individuals and dealing with outright rejections.

"But Megan, I am starting at 0. Zero customers, zero followers, zero dollars. How do I validate an idea when I have no one to ask?"

Excellent question, dear reader.

Here's the answer: you infiltrate the system you want to be in and methodically develop a Minimum Viable Product based on what you find. In other words, you start with a bare bones but effective product that solves a specific problem for the customer with whom you've become stalker-adjacent to.

Let's break it down to something that sounds less "covert ops" and more actionable. When you're starting at 0 as we all do (side note: always keep that in mind! Don't compare your Day 1 to someone else's Day 3,454), you'll need to do your research and find opportunities to develop a Minimum Viable Product, or MVP, to begin your test.

That means going out into the marketplace and becoming part of the community you want to sell to.

Creating a new makeup and skincare line? Get involved in MUA (make-up artist) groups or subreddits (what sections on reddit.com are called) where skincare and makeup addicts convene.

Becoming a fitness coach? Start commenting on Instagram influencers who promote clean living, or start becoming active in bodybuilding forums.

Want to become an Influencer on social media? Start researching YouTube vloggers or IGTV episodes made by other influencers and become a frequent contributor to their accounts.

The trick to all of this is to contribute and become a known person in the industry while keeping your eyes and ears open for low-hanging fruit that can become an easy entry point into your marketplace.

Consider Stephenie Meyer, who wrote the Twilight series. It started as fanfic on a forum where she had clout because she was a regular commenter, and she developed an audience that allowed her to create Twilight and have a die-hard fan base before she published a single book. We need to create your Twilight fans now.

One thing I want to emphasize: You will need to *contribute in earnest* and not just sell sell sell. The goal is to be seen as a valuable person to the community who knows their stuff. People are more likely to buy from someone they trust, and you don't want to lose that trust by coming in as a sales jerk right in the beginning.

Keep looking out for phrases like "wouldn't it be awesome if..." "I really wish there was a...." "[Product] is okay, but it doesn't...." See the opportunities here? This is where you build your product that solves these problems.

CHAPTER 5: THE NITTY (AND RARELY GRITTY) DETAILS

Now that you've decided what you want your business to be, it's time to make it official.

Let me start by saying, though, that you should absolutely consult professionals who are familiar with the laws of your city/state/country/continent/planet so that they can guide you through the oh-so-fun nuances that come along with dealing with your government.

Types of Businesses

Sole Proprietorship/DBA

This is the easiest to do and can be good for independent consultants, service-based freelancers, or smaller businesses. If you're operating under your own name, you're automatically considered a sole proprietor. If you plan to use a name other than your own, you'll most likely have to register a DBA, or, "Doing Business As." Sole proprietorships are usually linked to your personal information, like your Social Security number (in the US).

Corporations

These are better for product-based businesses, and larger entities as they have more layers of protection for your personal assets than a sole prop does, but there are stringent rules for keeping that "corporate veil" down so always consult with an accountant about which is going to work best for you.

1. LLC - Limited Liability Corporations which are good starting off points for partnerships or multi-person companies or if you plan to have a lot of different lines of businesses, like a real estate developer would (which involves getting an Umbrella LLC but that's more high level than I'm comfortable trying to pretend I know how to explain)
2. B Corp - a newer classification that has a strict set of guidelines. B Corps are businesses that adhere to strict environmental regulations and, consequently, may receive tax benefits.
3. S Corp - sort of like an LLC. Frankly, I've found the LLC to be easier to navigate, so I don't deal in S Corps often.
4. C Corp - the big conglomerate businesses. Most entrepreneurs avoid this until absolutely necessary as taxing gets a little hinky when it comes to company profits and your own income.

Considerations You'll Have To...Uh...Consider

- Do you need a sales tax license?
- Do you need any other licenses?
- What sort of insurance does a business like yours need?
- How will you handle customer complaints/returns/etc.?
- What are your policies? Get these in writing and on your website before you launch or make your first sale.
- What is it you need your business to make so you can survive the first few months?
- How will you figure out your price points? (meganbrame.com/pricr/ is the tool I use)

- Who will be your customers?
- How will you reach them?
- What is the value that your business brings to the marketplace?

Things You'll Probably Need (In Order of "Everyone Needs" to "Might Be Unique to Your Situation")

- **Bookkeeping software** - I've used QuickBooks Self-Employed for years. You can usually get a deal if you have an Etsy seller account
- **Customer management system** - How will you keep track of your customers? You don't need anything hugely fancy and expensive like SalesForce, but you should have a system for keeping track of customers and their interactions with your business.
- **PO Box or business address that isn't your home** - Please don't give people your home address.
- **Business bank account** - I've found local, small banks and credit unions have the best deals for small businesses who are just starting out.
- **Payment processor** (Paypal, Stripe, Square, Your Bank, etc.)
- **Newsletter Software**
- **Social media accounts**
- **Business phone number** - You can get a Google Voice number for free or upgrade to a fancy 1-800 number through something like RingCentral
- **Dedicated workspace**
- **Product storage space/shipping setup space**

People You Should Hire (In order of

"RIGHT FREAKING NOW" to "Your Call")

- **Accountant** - I like mine because he swears and tells me the government is full of shit (these are my people)
- **Lawyer** - We have access to our business lawyer. I say "access" because I don't speak with him a ton and I'm slightly scared of him (it's never a good day when you have to call the lawyer, you know?), but he's around on an as-needed basis.
- **Virtual Assistant** - VAs, in my opinion, are clutch. They can handle scheduling, automating, social media stuff, project management, and lots more. VAs take a ton of work off of your hands and are the one person I would recommend keeping around no matter the stakes. You can find freelance VAs on sites like Upwork.com or OnlineJobs.ph.
- **Customer Service Rep or Community Manager** - Believe me when I say hiring a customer service rep was one of my best decisions. Relieve the anxiety that comes along with this so you can focus on growing your business.
- **Sales Person** - Someone better at sales than you are who can bring in business while you work on product development.
- **Social Media Manager** - but later. Like, much later. You should really handle this on your own in the beginning so you can get a feel for your customer base.
- **Shipping Manager** - When you're ready to let the business work without you in it (physical products only, of course).
- **Web Developer** - I have one on retainer who handles setting up new themes, WordPress updates, and whatever weird little glitch I notice now and again. I used to do this all myself, and it took so much time! My developer is on a retainer-style system, so he comes in whenever I need something, and I pay him based on that, rather than a full-time, regular position. Note: move this further up the list

if you're totally lost when it comes to building a basic site for your business. Most platforms like WordPress, Squarespace, or Shopify make this really easy to do, which is why I have Web Developer so far down the list.

- **Interns** - I'm usually anti-intern because I feel they can get abused easily, but I understand that there's a place for them in the world. The US Department of Labor website lists out specific rules for interns and what you can use them for, so I would recommend reading up ahead of time and getting a good understanding so you can stay compliant.

Phew, that's a long list of things to consider, I know! Before you feel like you're already filing for bankruptcy due to having to pay for all of this, remember that this is not a definitive list, and all of these do NOT need to be crossed off at the same time.

I'd recommend setting up these things first as the bare bones when you're ready to get started:

1. Find an accountant and lawyer
2. Register your business with the government
3. Set up your business bank account
4. Answer the "considerations" questions

CHAPTER 6: BECOME A FRIEMPETITOR

Let's talk about competitors.

First: Recognize that, unless you're some sort of wizard, you're going to enter a pre-existing marketplace, and with that comes other businesses who are carving out their own share of it. These will be your competitors with whom you'll sometimes become very familiar with (whether you want to or not).

Allow me to make the argument that you absolutely need to know your competitors because they will inevitably be your key to success, and not from a "destroy them all" way, but in a sincere "rising tide lifts all boats" sort of way.

I've used two portmanteaus (which is the BEST word, don't you think?) regularly in my writing that I feel are absolutely critical to embrace as an entrepreneur (but feel free to use your own words if these are just a little too hokey for you): Accountabili-buddy and Friempetitor.

Accountabilibuddy is the term I use to 1. Piss off Grammarly and 2. Define the role that someone is assigned in your circle that holds you accountable to your commitments and who asks you the hard questions so that you can move forward in your goals.

Friempetitors are those who are in your field with whom you may consider being direct competitors but are also your friends. Usually, in my experience, it starts with competitors who turn into friends and rarely the other way around (though to be fair I don't know of many who see their friend's entrepreneurial struggles and goes "hell yeah, sign me up for that kinda stress fest!").

The majority of those who I would consider my closest friends are those whom I met while in competition against them. One friend I actually met while she and I were waiting to each pitch the same client! It started off kinda awkward (neither of us got the account, for the record), but she became one of the best friends I had when we lived in Brooklyn.

I equate this type of relationship to being war buddies: you and this competitor are in a unique position in that you two understand the weird nuances that go into your line of work and thus are able to relate to each other in a way that few others outside the niche can.

Granted, not everyone in your "scene" will be warm and bubbly and open to talking shop and sharing information; frankly, it's their loss. Not (only) because I'm your business Mom and feel that you're special and amazing, but (also) because they are missing a crazy-good opportunity, and it's one I strongly advocate you embracing as an entrepreneur. Don't look at competitors as battles that must be won, but instead see them as people who understand your business in a way that others might not. There's a true beauty in becoming friends and opening up to your competitors that I hope you'll give a shot at trying to develop.

Things I've Learned from My Competitors (Direct and Indirect)

1. Suppliers information
2. Vendors and contact information
3. How to navigate the world of shipping pallets of product
4. Which buyers to avoid
5. Pricing tips
6. Contacts for press/media
7. Insurance recommendations

And so on.

I actually had a VERY successful soap company give me their *entire* business plan. Can you believe that level of generosity and openness? It still blows me away, and I am eternally grateful to them.

And that's just as a product-based business. As a blogger and coach, there have been tons I've learned about sponsorships, posting rates, apps/services, taxes, etc. The time I've saved embracing my competitors as friends is incalculable!

Before this sounds more one-sided, let me clarify that this will always be a two-way street! I've given off my sources and costs to many friends who have asked or needed help. Oddly enough, being so open to pulling back the curtain of my business actually showed me that my calling was teaching others the things I've learned and done, and that's what started my blog which then turned into a coaching practice, courses, and this book!

So how do you find your competitors who would be open and friendly? It's way easier than you might think,

1. **Go to where they are** - Granted, I've made some friempetitors online, but the majority of the truly "close" relationships I have been by coming together in person. When I lived in Brooklyn, most of these relationships were made at street fairs or events. I'd just walk up to their booth, introduce myself (say I was also a soap maker/chandler/etc.), and shoot the shit. My blogging friends I've met by going to blogger conferences and plopping down next to them at lunch, or before a class and just being friendly.

2. **Accept that not everyone is into it** - I haven't had a 100% success rate at making friends in my niche. There are some who see me as competition and competition only, and you may run into that, as well. Believe me (and my therapist) when I say that it's not

you, it's them. Don't take their insecurity personally. I said it's their loss.

3. **Engage them** - As with the start of any relationship, be genuinely interested in them and their businesses. But don't go overboard and push hard, it might scare them off. I knew of one person who was known for meeting people, overwhelming them with a brain dump, and then expecting the same back. She was a very transactional person and developed a reputation in the world as a person to be held at arm's length.

4. **Offer help if you see an angle** - This was usually my sweet spot: if I heard something that was a bit of a pain point for them, I'd try to commiserate or offer a solution (if they seemed open to wanting one). What usually happened was that I'd know a resource that might be of use, so I'd take their card and email them the info once I got home.

5. **Support their business** - No, you don't have to buy their products, but in this day and age, it helps to be a cheerleader with social media. I'd advise, though, that you use personal accounts rather than your business account to like or comment if possible, as some might see your engagement as a poor attempt at siphoning their customer base.

6. **Remember it's a relationship** - Friempetitors are still friends, they just happen to be in your niche. If you really do like them and feel a genuine connection, you should absolutely cultivate it. My best friempetitors know my husband, have watched our cats, seen me drunk (ugh), invited me to their house parties, and so on. The business part tends to become less of a prior-

ity; the longer we get to know one another.

To hammer it home one more time: if you have the opportunity to meet your competitors, I would absolutely recommend you do so and become genuine friends with them; it will serve everyone in the community better!

CHAPTER 7: MASTERY VS. PERFECTION

You've probably heard the theory by Malcolm Gladwell, which states that mastery of something requires 10,000 hours of practice to achieve. I think it ends up being something like 10 years of dedication towards that thing.

If you forgive the outdated meme reference, allow me to say *ain't nobody got time for that.*

I've known many in the entrepreneurial world, myself included, that have felt they're inadequate and incapable of handling the task of commanding a price in exchange for their skills/products/etc. It's peak Impostor Syndrome: the feeling that you're not "fit" to be in the position you currently find yourself. It hits all of us at one point (or many points), so I'd revisit the chapter about IS if you start to feel it creeping up on you.

Let's break down the barrier here and discuss what it is you'll need to do to open your business and charge a fee for the output your business produces.

The rundown on what a Minimum Viable Product really is

Releasing a minimum viable product isn't about piecemeal; that doesn't make sense. Instead, MVPs are more about starting with the basic idea, vetting it against your fan base, and then building on top of that.

Think of it like running a bakery. Your end goal is an entire shop full of pastries and delectables, right? But you'd drive yourself crazy trying to come up with recipes, packaging, and the funds to make it all happen. So instead, what you do is start with cupcakes. Once you get feedback from your customers on their favorite cupcakes, and you have learned what works and what doesn't, you start to make a cake based on that recipe. And then that cake sells out, like, all the time. So then you start to make another flavor, and you test that.

Pretty soon you're off to the races (er...whatever the bakery version of that would be), and you've got a full product line that you know will be profitable, because you've created it with your customers each step of the way, guiding you and steering you in the right direction.

So what are some of the ways people figure out if their MVP has legs? A couple of ways:

1. **They Pre-Sell.** One of the times I did a launch properly, I offered a pre-sale via IndieGoGo for a face care collection I was launching. This helped me see if it was going to be an actual collection that sold AND got me working capital. This is one of the best ways to determine if you're heading in a good direction, or if you need to start over again. Pre-selling is totally terrifying, I know, but it's less terrifying than figuring out how to pay the bills with a product that people won't buy.

2. **They survey their customers at each step.** Offer in-

centives for your customers if you need to, or just keep it to your VIP customers (I talk about how to do this with ConvertKit in my free webinar"Perfect Product Launch," which you can see at https://www.meganbrame.com/perfectproductlaunch). Ask them open-ended questions instead of yes/no so that you can figure out how to satisfy their needs.

3. **They keep it lean.** No fancy bells and whistles, no distractions. Successful small business owners start with the foundation, make sure that is good, and then build on top of it, like the skateboard in the above picture.

The first step to determine how to make the MVP is to figure out your original end game and work backward.

So if I were starting a new skincare company, I'd probably want to have products that cleanse my skin and maybe treat acne (or dry skin, etc.). So my MVP would be…an unscented soap. From there, I learn how that formula helps/hurts my customers. Is it too harsh? Does it have a good lather? From there, I begin to build, tweak, and perfect.

I don't launch with a collection of 17 different soaps, never knowing if ANY of them will work. I start with just one. It's simple, it's not fancy, but it's a good foundation, and it's the best way I learn how my product sells.

I've broken this down into a workbook that you can download for free in my Membership Library at MeganBrame.com/join-the-library/ but the crux of the matter is this: waiting for something to be perfect means you'll never launch. You have to be confident in the "good enough" and upgrade as you go.

MVPs are your MVP

I think the concept of Minimum Viable Product(s) or MVP(s) make a lot of new small business owners roll their eyes because it seems like such an unrealistic idea to have: why make something simple when I can make something amazing and perfect?

And then they fail because they waited for that "something" to be perfect.

It's never perfect. Not life, not your relationships, not your finances, and definitely not your products.

I know this all too well. I used to force myself to have ev.er.y.thing down to a T before I would launch a collection (and it was ALWAYS an entire collection, never just one product). The packaging had to be beautiful and just so, with precise details. The collection had to be fully fleshed out, and include multiple SKUs (sometimes in multiple scents). I'd throw hundreds and sometimes thousands of dollars into a collection that I thought was totally done. And then I'd launch it.

And wait. And wait. And see that credit card payment day comes closer and closer without any sales.

Most of my launches would be considered…maybe not failures outright, but they definitely took more work to recoup my costs than I would've liked. Some, yes, okay, were total money pits and took me a long time to recover.

I did this over and over again, never knowing what the hell was wrong. It took me many years for the slap in the face to come that showed me what I had been doing wrong the entire time.

Here's the answer: I didn't involve my fans in the launch at all. I was throwing up a collection, thinking I knew best when I knew nothing at all.

So, my darling baby business owner, you are here to learn from my mistakes, yes? So this is probably one of the biggest lessons I can teach you:

You cannot launch a perfect product. If you want to succeed, you must launch a "good enough" product. This is known as a Minimum Viable Product or an MVP.

Now What About Mastery?

So now that we've gotten rid of the stigma of needing to be perfect let's get back to the 10,000 hours bit.

To me, "Mastery" equates to being able to understand something well enough that you can talk about it ad nauseum without stopping. I wouldn't say I'm a Master when it comes to making sure liquid eyeliner doesn't end up all over my face or upgrading bathroom fixtures. For many things, I am a full-time student at the academy of YouTube. The hours of videos I've watched on so many topics makes YouTube both a blessing and a curse (want to learn everything ever? Now you can!) and has shown me how little I know on so many topics.

I would say, though, that I'm a Master at marketing. I say that with full confidence even though it sounds a little gloat-y in my head, but damn it, we've all got to be good at something! (And for the record, I am a Master at marketing, but I'm not perfect!)

I know my calling is marketing because I talk about it whenever I get the chance. I know because I could go into senior position job interviews and Board meetings with absolute confidence that I knew what I was doing, and was confident enough to say "I don't know, but I can find out" when I was unsure. I began to know intrinsically in my gut when something wasn't right in a marketing campaign, and I would fight to fix it. I never had that level of fight in me for anything else, and I'm sure to an outsider, the hills I've died on have probably seemed a little strange, but marketing is something I am passionate about and feel needs to be championed.

That paragraph was going to be way longer, but I made myself stop. See? I can't help talking about why marketing is amazing!

I once told my therapist during a session that "I know two things to be true in my life: my marriage is strong, and I'm good at what I do." Then, you know, the rest of the session talked about everything I wasn't good at. Um, but I digress.

I didn't wake up with an uncanny understanding of sales funnels and value-based initiatives, though. It took me years of study, trial, and error, and pivoting to find this place where I have a breathtaking level of confidence in my skills.

My degree was in Social Science(s. I'm still not sure if it's singular or plural since I lost my degree during a move) with concentrations on psychology, sociology, and history...which means the degree itself was pretty much useless and had nothing to do directly with marketing or business. I see now that the skills I learned with it were a natural fit for where I would end up, but at the time "Temple, Icon, and Deity in India" didn't really feel like it had much to do with my job situation (amazing class, by the way).

My point is this: Mastery comes at a gradual pace and not

from some lightning strike to your brain like the movie Phenomenon. But there are ways to hack it a little to get to where you need to be.

First thing: Who cares?

Why should you care to master the niche in which you'll open a business? Maybe that's a "duh" question, but just in case: Your goal for your business should be to command a price that pays your bills and offers you a chance to achieve your goals, whatever they are. Freedom to travel because your business is making money when you're not there? The ability to quit your day job and do what you love? The chance to be recognized as "great?"

Whatever your goals are, your business should work to open the lane that gets you there. It can't do that if you're undercharging or trying to beat your competitors to the bottom of the market. You need to charge what you're worth, and mastery gives you the ability to defend that to both the outside world and your inner Negative Nancy.

How to Achieve Mastery in Your Field

1. **Be open to others** - I learned the foundations of marketing through podcasts I would listen to while I was filling orders in my soap business. Amy Porterfield, Tim Ferriss, and Pat Flynn podcasts were staples of my playlists, and they were clutch giving me an understanding of what I needed to be doing and why. Let go of the ego and allow yourself to learn from others in your field. It could be a competitor, an industry leader, or anyone else you feel has something to teach you. Don't wall yourself up from the world and pretend you can't learn from others who are doing the same thing you are.

2. **Be voracious** - My husband is a writer and a lover of fiction. He consumes new books at a breathtaking speed, and it rarely matters the genre (he's not huge into Sci-Fi). I'm similar, except I am a nerd for non-fiction and can clear my library's "Personal Development" section out all on my own. When you know the field you want to open a business in, you have to love it and want everything that field has to offer. Keep learning, reading, listening, and keep loving it.

3. **Don't let a lack of [insert-insecurity-here] stop you** - You're not going to be a Master on Day 1, and that is 400% fine. Allow yourself to be a student and an entrepreneur in your niche and adjust as you go. The longer you wait because of [insert insecurity here], the lower the chance you'll ever get to Day 1 at all.

4. **Give it to the world for free** - look, I am NOT someone who believes a successful business gives things away, but I make an exception when it comes to knowledge. I've learned so much because of the "gurus" in my world who have published hours of podcast episodes or encyclopedic volumes of blog posts that I am eternally indebted to them, and I continue to pay it forward with my own blog, podcasts, and webinars that are totally free. When you've begun to feel confident in your niche, it's time to break out that knowledge and give it to the world. Write a blog post, go on a podcast, make a video, whatever method you feel most comfortable with and launch it out to the public. Consider it a good marketing tactic that just happens to be altruistic!

To me, the last point is clutch in achieving Mastery, and

here's why: I originally said that I believe a level of Mastery is achieved when you're able to not shut up about the niche you're in. Publishing the lessons you've learned will give you a level of confidence that will let you slip into the title of Master, and the more you give out, the more your followers will see you that way.

And remember: it won't ever be perfect. Let go of the need for perfection and find the freedom of infinite growth, upgrades, and learning.

One final note: You might be thinking you already know the product/service you want to create and simply need to find the audience to sell it to. That's fine, and this strategy can be used to build the platform to sell it, but if you're building something without knowing the audience, at least consider the idea that the product/service might need to be more fluid than originally thought until you find through testing that it will become successful.

CHAPTER 8: ONE HOUR A DAY

Coming home from your day job can be pretty exhausting. There have been times where I've come home from work and felt unable to move off of the couch. It became physically exhausting, and I had a desk job! There were nights when I would come home and have plenty of time to do something, *anything*, in my business, but I just couldn't.

You know why? My business was like a mountain, and I was at basecamp with a cramp in my leg. Everything felt daunting and immediate, so I would just shut down and do nothing.

Do you know that I had two months' worth of video shot for my blog, and it just sat on my SD card? I felt like I couldn't devote the time to editing all of that video, it would take forever, and I just want to sit and, I don't know, marinate in my exhaustion and buy stuff on Amazon. (It took me 2 hours when I finally got it all done, and I was shocked how quickly that actually took.)

That is a One Day mentality, not a Day 1! Success, of any kind, doesn't come in an avalanche. It comes with tiny, incremental movements. Every second you've spent on your business, even if it's just reading this, is one more second that you've moved forward.

That's no excuse to rest on your laurels (though I do appreciate you taking the time to read this!) but instead is a motivation to keep you going. Now that you've spent one second thinking about your business do that again tomorrow. And the next day.

And every day for the rest of the week.

One second feels laughable, right? What's one *blip* of activity going to do that benefits you? Maybe a second is a little too ridiculous, but were you consistently working on your business for one second every day before? Or was it just a thought that came in and out of your head, especially on bad days when you wanted to rage quit?

Here's my point: Working towards a goal, any goal, means dedicating a consistent effort to making it happen. If all you can give is one second of attention, but you can give it every day for a consistent amount of time, then you're training yourself to develop a plan of action.

The true goal, now that we're past one second is to work on 3,600 of those seconds and dedicate one hour every day on your business.

If you're a crazy perfectionist and feel like one hour isn't going to accomplish everything you want to do, remember that it's one hour that actually created a *positive* output. If you want to keep going after that hour, that's up to you, but don't feel like you need to until you're really in an established groove of consistency.

What One Hour a Day Does for You and Your Business

Creates a Plan for Movement
Developing a habit like setting aside a specific time for business planning offers you the opportunity to determine which path is the most beneficial for your success. Another way to put this is one hour a day causes you to be proactive on your business instead of reactive (and playing catch-up)

Practices Intentionality

Along those lines, one hour a day also forces you to take intentional actions for your business. Rather than just thinking and acting on the fly, time blocking 5 hours a week helps you get into a "work" mindset. If you've ever been able to develop a habit of going to the gym and sticking to it (respect), you know what I'm talking about.

Gains Perspective

A frustration that can come with this is "what am I going to do ev.er.y. day?" There's a fear of monotony or boredom that might come with this, and let's be honest, that's a logical fear.

However, the repetition that comes along with time blocking can make you take a new look at something that you previously thought was finished. For example, I have a course called 'Gram Crackers, which is about marketing on Instagram. At first, I created it to be rudimentary, like a 101 to Instagram Business class, but it wasn't my thing, and frankly, it wasn't selling.

I thought about closing it for a long time but damn it, and I loved the name. I kept thinking about it for a few weeks and came to the realization that I knew what to do with it: refresh the course with what I'm good at marketing!

Rather than giving up on the class, I rewrote it as an advanced marketing class that teaches how to create sales funnels and improves community engagement on Instagram. Now the class isn't beholden to whatever overnight changes Instagram rolls out, which made it a pain to update. Instead, it teaches ways to utilize the benefits of social media engagement to your advantage, and I'm much happier with it.

The new path for Gram Crackers wouldn't have happened if I just scrapped it, which would've been a huge loss! I kept picking at it and shifted the focus to find what it needed to succeed, and that's thanks to time blocking.

Makes Learning a Priority

Even if you hate reading (what are you doing here?), time-blocking forces you to become a learner. Rare is the person who knows everything about running a business

You don't know what you don't know, and each time you work on your business, you open the door to new education. Maybe you're ready to register your business with the government but don't know which business structure would be the best, so you have to research. Or you really have no idea how to edit your photos in Lightroom but want to learn, so you take a class on Lynda or something like that. Time blocking takes out the "no time to learn" and forces you to expand your skill sets in order to move forward.

Provides the Opportunity to Experiment

Along the same lines as "Gains Perspective," the repetitiveness of time blocking each week will give your mind a chance to stretch and see things in a new angle, which could lead to trying new and exciting things. This book is an example of that! I was writing content for my blog when I thought that I'd love to expand some of the topics into a book that helps others make the leap into creating a business. Maybe it wouldn't work out, but writing it would be a good thought experiment, and maybe it'd be something I'd enjoy!

Let's set up a plan for your Power Hour (not the drinking kind):

How to Create a Consistent Effort Towards a Goal

1. **Write it down**

    Keeping things in your head doesn't do you any favors. To really understand what the completion of a goal actually looks like, you're going to need to see the fully fleshed-out idea on paper. Brainstorm by writing down or draw ideas as they come, or cut out pictures to create a vision board; whatever best encapsulates how you can process the information is the route you should pick. But be specific, and don't let yourself off the hook with vague statements. "I want to be rich!" doesn't work. "I want to earn an annual net income of $1 million" is better.

2. **Schedule it**

Nothing works without a plan, and a plan doesn't work without giving it due time. Set aside specific times each week and stick to it. Think of it like going to school or the gym: dedicating specific time helps you develop a habit towards learning and effective goal achievements. Dedicating a set schedule will help you develop better focus and get into a routine of specific work towards getting what you want.

3. **Work backward**

So you want to earn $1 million in net income as your yearly salary, what does it take to get to that point? At an annual salary of $1 million, you'll need to pull in about $19,231 per week in income.

Okay: to get your income to $19,231/week, how many sales will you need to make, and how much should you charge for each of your products or services? (Side note: I have a great workbook that can help you with this: https://www.meganbrame.com/pricr/ [no "e"]) Work backward from your ultimate goal to help establish milestones and work out realistic timelines. The keyword is "realistic" here! Don't expect to reach it quickly, easily, or both. Give yourself time to achieve, allow for setbacks (it happens), windfalls, etc.

4. **Set yourself up for success (remove distractions)**

Use apps that limit your time spent on websites invest in tools that help keep you focused, download meditation music, avoid social media, whatever you have to do to move forward. Also, don't allow yourself to fall prey to the "me, too!" (not #metoo) mentality.

It's very easy to get into the comparison game, especially with everyone broadcasting their wins on social media. Don't get caught up in comparing your Day 1 to someone else's Day 45,673, or even the Day 1, they might be showing you on Instagram. Very few things are unfiltered out there, so keep your eyes on your own paper and recognize that not everything is always as it appears with your role models, idols, or competitors.

5. **Keep a Why close by**

There are days that are going to suck; it's just the way things are. I'm pretty sure that the reason people keep pictures of their family on their desks at work is to prevent them from rage quitting every day as it helps to remind them why they're attending yet ANOTHER meeting about a meeting. I recommend you do the same: keep a token around that reminds you quickly of the good parts in your life and the reason why you want this goal in the first place.

6. **Write down what you've accomplished**

I cannot take credit for this, though I wish I could. I first heard of the "Jar of Awesome" from Tim Ferriss' podcast, and I immediately embraced it. Get a jar or bowl and a stack of Post-Its. Every time you get a win, whether it's wee or large, write it down, fold it, and drop it into the Jar of Awesome. This is SO important, as it's a quantifiable amount of things that have moved you forward and is a great, tangible reminder of the things you've accomplished (and the amount of things!) that can be clutch to have around on bad days.

So often we get caught in the trenches and the day-to-day slog of working on our businesses that we forget how far we've come. The Jar of Awesome helps to remind you of how incredible you are!

Now just do that 5 days a week. This is known, un-creatively, as the "5 Hour Rule" and is a proven way that many successful entrepreneurs (Warren Buffet, Bill Gates, Benjamin Franklin) have managed their time.

The "science" behind this is that by intentionally setting aside a set amount of time each day, you begin to build habits of prioritizing and acting with a deliberate effort towards your goal. This book was written on that principle, I blocked out 3 - 4 pm Monday through Friday and created a goal of at least 30 pages a week. Was it a grind? Sometimes, definitely! There were days when the last thing I wanted to do was fire up Google Docs and try to fill pages, but it got done, nonetheless. I put on my headphones and hunkered down for 60 minutes every day.

"Megan, I'm *super* happy (sarcastically) that you get to spend time at work doing stuff like this, but I have a grueling schedule and have to deal with kids/family/work/tv shows/gym/another excuse."

Real talk: If one hour a day seems out of your grasp, then entrepreneurship isn't for you. If there's something you truly want in your life, you'll find a way to make it happen.

Grinding out an hour of your time 5 days a week is a small start and is absolutely critical towards setting your sights towards becoming a successful entrepreneur. Any excuse (unless you're comatose or something) is just that, an excuse.

Have to work weird hours? Do an hour before or after work. Have kids? Work during their nap time or when they go to bed. Becoming Amish and getting rid of the Internet? Read more business books and write down what you've learned.

I'm sympathetic that everyone has a different path in life, but this is the one rule I refuse to budge on when it comes to starting Day 1. Once you get that your undivided attention needs to be given towards moving forward, then you begin to see the fruits of your hard work and the sacrifice of that hour a day.

Okay, now that we got those negative vibes out of the way, let's talk about what the hell you should do during that hour.

How to Spend Your Hour a Day

The good part of this is that most business things can count towards your one hour. Some days you might not feel driven to push hard, and that is totally fine. Remember, it's the small steps that add up to big changes. But if you're thinking "I don't even know where to start," here are some ideas:

- Read a business book
- Research trends in your industry
- Research competitors
- Work on your branding strategy
- Draft content for social media and/or marketing
- Listen to a business podcast
- Watch videos from successful entrepreneurs (Gary Vee, Tim Ferriss, etc.)
  Research shows, conferences, events
- Develop your budget

- Work on component sourcing (if product-based: what will you need to make your product? If service: what tools will help streamline your business?)
- Work on delegate/eliminate/automate (more on that later)
- Bookkeeping
- Customer engagement
- Take a class
- Product photography
- Editing products/photos
- Work on an editorial calendar
- What do you anticipate will be your busiest quarter? How can you front-load work to make it less stressful?
- Pitch potential clients
- Pitch editors stories for press clippings

I could go on, but then this would be a book of lists and not actions! You get the point though, and there are a plethora of things that "count" towards one hour a day.

As an aside, don't let yourself fall into what I call "productivity guilt." This was something I had to work out in therapy as I felt time that wasn't spent being "productive" (earning money) was time wasted, and I felt hours where I could list something I had "worked on" were the only ones worth mentioning. Yoga? Pfft, who has time for that? Meditation? How could I look myself in the mirror knowing that I spent an hour sitting quietly when I could've been working?

Self-care was never considered "productive" to me, and consequently, I took horrible care of myself. Self-care is something I have to work on still intentionally (another "one hour a day" part of my life), and business-self-care is something you should consider, as well.

Never feel like doing something passive, like reading a

business book or watching videos, is "cheating" and isn't productive. These things are only counter-productive if you're actively using them to avoid doing something else. But if you spend 5 hours next week solely listening to a marketing-based podcast because you know very few things about marketing, then that totally counts, and I ain't mad about it.

Never feel like YOUR one hour a day has to be comparable to someone else's and don't avoid business-self-care things that look like leisure to outsiders. Learning about business is one of the most important aspects of success, after all!

CHAPTER 9: DODGE, DIP, DUCK, DIVE, AND DODGE

The title of this chapter is brought to you by the fantastic movie *Dodgeball: A True Underdog Story*.

When it comes to running your own business, to be successful, you'll have to learn how to take hits, be flexible, and adjust your plan. The way you expect things to go, unfortunately, is rarely how it ends up going.

Some things will end up like potholes, little annoyances that mess up your alignment but are solvable. Other things end up becoming giant downed trees across the road, impossible to navigate through. This chapter is going to cover how you solve both of those scenarios, and probably everything in between.

The first thing I would ask of you is that you accept that the way you see your business and how you envision it succeeding will most likely not be the way it actually does. I don't say that to disappoint you, but instead to give you a freedom that few people experience: you'll now have the ability to understand that there's a fluidity to this and your ability to embrace that will set you miles ahead of any potential competitors.

So let's dive into the flow, shall we?

What Happens When It Doesn't Go According to Plan (Potholes)

I'm not sure why I'm continuing with a driving analogy, so just stick with me here.

My personal and professional life has hit me with many a pothole. My little body car is driving down the road, enjoying life, and suddenly I'm completely shaken up. A pothole I hadn't seen coming threw me off my flow and rattled me to my core. I look in my rear view mirror, trying to figure out how that happened, but I keep going forward (sometimes to a mechanic to get a full alignment readjustment. I guess in this scenario that'd be a business coach or therapist.)

I've been laid off from a job that I had invested in emotionally way more than I had ever done for a corporate gig, I've had "sure thing" sales turn into ghosts, I've had product launches that went absolutely nowhere. All of these I'd consider being potholes: they affected me hard for a solid moment in time, but I kept going forward as I tried to figure out if there was something I missed before hitting the hole.

To me, business potholes are things that you can recognize to be a momentary shake-up, a red blip on the radar. They absolutely positively suck, but they do go away, and you can work through them.

To get past a pothole, even if it's a ginormous crater, takes a great amount of self-confidence and almost Teddy Roosevelt-ian levels of blind willingness to keep going forward. When you come to a pothole on your business road, you're going to need to utilize a great amount of self-care and reflection to make it through, but you will make it.

What are some examples of potholes you might run over? There's no guarantee will encounter these, but the more specific examples I can give you, the more we can take away their power to stop you from reaching your goals, so let's list some out:

- Bad PR/Loud and unreasonable customers with social media accounts
- Violation of federal/state/local laws that you're ignorant to (I have a story about this!)
- Large orders lost or damaged in the mail (please always get insurance. I learned this the hard way)
- Accusations of copying another business, whether intentional or not
- Running out of money but needing to pay for something that's mission-critical
- Having employees quit abruptly
- Having a "talk" with your spouse or significant other about money
- Another Great Recession
- Having things or ideas get stolen by a customer, vendor, or client
- Running out of ideas for content, services, or products
- Feeling like you're an impostor in your business
- Feeling like you're working for nothing with no end in sight
- Sudden medical expenses that take you away from your business
- Another COVID-19

Potholes can be temporary setbacks in your business that don't completely throw you off the path but instead test your resolve to go forward. You can absolutely hate them when you hit them, but if you don't let them stop you from continuing on your path, you'll come out stronger and with a new understanding of what you're capable of doing.

Potholes can also be a warning that you may need to take stock of your goals and why they're affected by this event. They have value in their ability to make you check yourself and prevent small blips from turning into big catastrophes.

Okay, I think I've bummed us out enough, so let me tell you about the time the FDA almost tried to shut me down:

I was at my second ever trade show, the Natural Products Expo in Baltimore, MD. I was up in the "New Products" section, which essentially gave me a table and some pipe and drape (way different from the aesthetic requirements of other industry trade shows I've been to), so for me, the expectations were low. I made the booth really stand out as best I could and was actually having a really great show!

I was passing out soap samples and saw a guy come my way with a clipboard. He just looked like some kinda buyer for a store and was a little lost, so I smiled and offered him a soap sample. He took the sample, put it in his shirt pocket, then looked at his clipboard.

Him: "Oh, Metropolis Soap Company, I know you!"
Me: "Oh, really?" *getting excited*
Him: "Yes. My name is [redacted mostly because I can't remember], and I'm from the FDA. Here's my card."
Me: *frozen smile on my face, panic in my stomach* "Hi."
Him: "I've been to your website, we have some issues you need to correct."
Me: *annoyed he took the soap sample*

It was an absolutely terrifying moment that was caused by me saying that tea tree oil has astringent properties (I used it in a facial soap), which the FDA does not recognize as being true. He gave me a stern warning, told me to change the verbiage on my website, then left.

With my soap sample.

That I made to entice new businesses to try my product and order for their store, not for government employees who had no buying power whatsoever. Sigh.

I had no clue the FDA didn't believe in the astringent properties of tea tree oil (nor did I ever imagine the freaking FDA would be looking at my little website), but it didn't matter; I was in violation of federal law and as such could've been subject to serious fines and penalties. Maybe that soap sample ended up saving me, after all! I did change the verbiage on my website and avoided mentioning anything remotely beneficial about essential oils except for their scents.

Lesson learned, pothole overcome.

What Happens When A Roadblock Completely Stops You in Your Tracks

Roadblocks are bigger, scarier, and more breathtaking than potholes.

They will scare the ever-loving crap out of you and make you wonder whether or not you're going to continue being in business at all.

I'm sure you can imagine some serious events that would prevent you from moving forward in your business goals so that I won't list any out there (okay two: Hating the business you've put your heart into. Or the IRS citing you for tax evasion. Only one of these has happened to me!), but there are things in your business life that will make you have to reroute your entire path.

Roadblocks have their purpose, though you might not see it at the time (well, maybe you see why the IRS is coming after you); they are a boon to your ability to run a successful business. Roadblocks just show you that you're not on the right path and that you need to rethink things.

The roadblock that happened to me was growing to hate my business that I had poured SO much time, effort, and money into (sorry if you thought it was the IRS. Like the WuTang Clan, the IRS ain't nothing to eff with, and so I don't). I talk about it more in other chapters of this book, but that roadblock made me answer some tough questions that signaled both the end of my business and the beginning of an entirely new journey...the journey that gave me the opportunity to talk to you right now!

Your Emergency First Aid Kit

Now that we've accepted that business life won't always be sunshine and puppies let's actually lay out how you can get past a pothole and around a roadblock.

Knowledge

Even if you're brand new to the industry you've chosen, you're still way ahead of someone who has no idea what your industry even is. To overcome a pothole with knowledge, you'll need to open yourself up to being confident in your skills and abilities.

When I was laid off, I knew that I would get a new job quickly because I was a talented marketer with a resume that included NYC startups and large non-profits, and that looks mighty shiny and fancy when applying to jobs in a small town. I was confident in my ability to showcase my talent because I had acquired a boatload of marketing skills that gave me a leg up. I got another job within a month (which I then left to go back to full-time self-employment, but I digress)!

Knowledge can help you navigate around roadblocks, too. When there's something in your path that is so significant and awesome (like, the actual definition of awesome, not the "totally, dude!" Version) that it prevents you from moving forward, your acquired skills and expertise will help you understand the significance of what you're facing and give you the opportunity to adjust as needed.

Experience

Similar to knowledge, but different in that you have most

likely already dealt with something in your life much more serious than this.

When you hit a pothole that shakes you, you'll need to take some time to recoup and take yourself out of the situation. Once you're able to take a step back and get a bigger picture of what's going on, you'll most likely notice a similarity to something else you've faced in life before. You overcame that challenge, so you have the experience to make it past this pothole, too.

Roadblocks can be navigated with experience, too. When you hit a roadblock and can't move forward, you'll need to use the experiences that have brought you to this point and use them as signals to help you figure out where to go next.

When I realized I couldn't go on running the business I had spent a decade building, I spent a lot of time reflecting on the choices I made that got me there. I refused help because I thought I couldn't afford it. I put myself in a self-fulfilling prophecy loop that said I couldn't sell it because I didn't make sales, and I didn't make sales because I couldn't sell. I couldn't give up control of any aspect because I wanted to look impressively busy due to my own insecurities.

Releasing those experiences from my subconscious made me realize that I had made a lot of mistakes that I could chock up to stubbornness and fear, but if I did it, then I knew other people would, too, so I could take those experiences and help prevent others from hitting the same roadblock I did. I hit the roadblock of hating my business and used the experiences that had got me there to pivot and drive down a new, better path.

Someone else who understands what you're going through

Misery absolutely loves the company, and no one knows that better than business war veterans.

To get past a pothole, you're going to have to step outside of your comfort zone and make friends with your competitors (see my chapter on Accountabilibuddies for help) because they might be able to help you move past it in a way that makes sense for your industry. Don't rely on advice from your friend who has no idea what it's like to be in your niche because as well-intentioned as their advice might be; it just might not be the right puzzle piece that fits in the spot.

To overcome a roadblock is going to require something a little more intensive. Roadblocks rarely happen unexpectedly; there's usually a sign or two before that lets you know this area is prone to falling rocks or a high wind warning that you know could take down an old tree. But if you failed to miss those signs, you're going to need to dig deep and find out why.

This is where your "mechanic" comes into play. I mean, not your actual mechanic, unless they're really prophetic, but your life mechanic: a therapist or a business coach, though I prefer you have both.

A therapist is going to help you find the source of these blind spots in your life so that you can work on seeing them for what they are. A business coach (or marketing, financial, etc. coach) is going to help you take that knowledge and apply it to the specific blocks in your business. At what point did you realize there was no moving forward in your business, and how can we utilize that so we never do it again? Professionals trained for this type of work are absolutely essential, and you should absolutely take advantage of them when you feel like there's no way to move ahead.

A Plan

Lastly, but not least, you're going to need to figure out what happens next and lay that out in as much detail as possible.

Potholes are a warning sign that your business isn't as shored up as you originally thought. They remind you to revisit your original plan and goals and see if you're going off track. Potholes are an opportunity to correct issues and get ahead of the possible catastrophe.

Roadblocks let you know that it's time to re-evaluate your entire plan and figure out where you go next. It may involve you completely scrapping your original idea and moving on, for which you'll need to create a new plan but now with more knowledge and experience.

Both potholes and roadblocks give you an immensely valuable opportunity to become more flexible in your business and with your goals. Sometimes your plan may be too vague and need to be expanded; other times, you might realize you've made some poor assumptions on how this was going to go.

Regardless of the road ahead, being flexible and embracing the flow for the life of your business can mean the difference between being an entrepreneur, or being a One Day-er.

CHAPTER 10: STAY THE COURSE AND KEEP YOUR FOCUS

Let me talk to you about pens.

My Mom was and still is a voracious pen hoarder, and that's one of the qualities I've inherited from her. However, my pen obsession is very specific: Inc R2 Precision Ballpoint Pens.

I love them because the ink is free-flowing, so it ends up looking like a nicer gel pen. You would think my obsession with these doesn't make sense, because I'm left-handed so if I start writing in a frenzy (which...is there any other way?) my writing inevitably becomes smeared, and the bottom of my left-hand gets a mustache of ink, but I can't help it, I love those pens.

I was reading *Girl, Stop Apologizing* by Rachel Hollis, and it was a chapter about drinking water or something. The subject isn't important except to say it had nothing to do with pens or writing. My mind began to wander while I read as it invariably does (and as yours might be right now, too. I understand!), and I started thinking about how I missed writing in my journal. I used to write in it every night and, truth be told, that was my most successful time in 2019 both financially and psychologically, so for the record: start writing in a journal.

Anyhow, I was thinking about this and realized why I

hadn't been writing lately: I had lost the pen that went in the little pen holder of my journal. I had taken it with me on a flight (notebook and pen are absolute staples of my travel gear), came home, unpacked, and had no idea where it went.

A sane person would say, "it's not about the pen, Megan. Use a damn Bic and call it a day," and I would totally agree with your rationality. Except I **need** my R2 pen. I need the way it feels on the thick paper of my journal. I like the way my handwriting looks with it, like some sort of old-timey land deed. I like the feeling it gives me as I write in my journal.

So I went searching for my pen. At first, I looked in the usual places: pen cup #1 on my desk, pen cup #2 on my bulletin board, space under my monitor....and then it just went full-on Crazy-Town where I was tearing apart my office looking for this one single pen, while all of the other perfectly fine pens and pencils sat in their cup, feeling rejected.

I ended up finding it underneath my bedside table, but before that, I was seriously considering whether I was really going to tell my husband that I had to go to Target at 8:45 pm because I needed a single very specific pen in our house full of perfectly fine other pens.

So now that you know I'm an insane person, let me get to the point of this story: there are times in life and in business, where you'll fixate on the most-perfect tool that will solve all of your problems. You cannot envision going onward without this perfect tool; nothing else will do and damn anyone for thinking you sound like a crazy person for needing it.

Except that tool isn't the thing that solves your problem. You just think it will.

My R2 pen, which isn't a fancy pen (I mean, I got my first one at the Dollar Store) and doesn't do anything amazing but write well, was the thing I fixated on as THE main block that was preventing me from getting back into journaling.

But really, it wasn't the pen - it was the excuse that I didn't *have* the pen, which allowed me to forego my journaling that day. I became obsessed with finding that pen and wasted so much time, time that I could've spent writing a few paragraphs in my journal and feeling satisfied. Instead, I avoided the task by making an excuse and moving my focus towards finding the R2 pen.

I've seen this happen with other entrepreneurs, too. So many of us become enraptured with the idea that something out there will solve a major problem for us, we just have to find it and then the clouds will open and rain money and happiness down upon our heads.

We seek out this tool or app, or we overhaul our branding and packaging or hire/fire someone on a whim because we need change, but we never address the real issue. We move our focus away from the problem and instead try to find band-aids that will cover it and let us move away from the uncomfortable work of digging in and working through the issues.

I didn't want to write in the journal because I didn't really know what to say. Should I address why I had been avoiding it for so long? Should I just pick right back up as nothing happened? Why was I making such a big deal of this in the first place?

I've done the same in my business. My soap company changed names twice and branding/aesthetics nearly once a year. I went from Pulp Horror to Whole Foods Natural to Black Old Timey Goth and everywhere in between. I thought that changing things up would bring me the success I felt was so elusive when the truth was that my business WAS successful, I just wasn't ever confident in my own choices and felt FOMO when looking at other companies.

Looking back, I wouldn't have changed my path because it got me here talking to you, but I can see that there were some serious avoidance issues that I was dealing with, and unfortunately, they aren't unique to me.

There are going to be times in your business where you get this itch to change things up to help you move to the next level, and that is totally fine! You should start to worry, though, if you become fixated on finding that one magic pill...because there *is* no magic pill. What there is instead is an avoidance of resolving a problem that involves hard work.

Switching out my aesthetic every year let me avoid digging into why I was afraid to ask for the sale; it wasn't my skills as a salesperson or my self-confidence, no, it was the way the packaging looked.

Changing your customer base from exclusively B2B to B2C might not be because of the marketplace, it might be because you have some inferiority stuff to work out and are afraid to go for the big business.

Scrapping your coaching business and working on physical products might not be because you're a bad coach, it might be because you're not promoting that vertical of your business correctly because you're afraid of the responsibility to coach someone and don't want to seem pushy.

Do you see what I'm getting at? Change in business can absolutely be good, and I am not recommending you stay in the same spot for years. If, however, you feel like a scorched earth policy might be best while you move onto something new, allow me to ask that you do the hard work first and figure out what's going on that's truly bringing this feeling on.

Talk with a business coach, Accountabilibuddy, therapist, or anyone in your life who can truly listen to you and offer feedback on what they hear before you make drastic changes. I've run into enough entrepreneurs who have let their personal insecurities leak into their businesses that have had serious ramifications to their progress, and I don't want that for you, which is why I had to include a chapter about it.

This isn't a book about therapy, I know. But if you're going to run a business that is an extension of you that holds meaning and is something you choose to devote your time to, it goes without saying that you might run into some self-inflicted roadblocks that give you permission to lose your focus.

I've called this both "The Honeymoon Phase" and "Shiny Object Syndrome" and am guilty of running into these walls dozens of times where I'll lose enthusiasm for a project and let it fall by the wayside in favor of something newer and "better." It rarely is "better" and is instead an entirely new set of problems, so now I try to recognize it for what it is and work out the issue. Here's how I usually combat these blocks:

How to Get Past Shiny Object Syndrome (SOS)

1. **Identify the Issue** - Take a step back and try to look at what you're trying to accomplish here. Is SOS letting you avoid having uncomfortable conversations with yourself or others because you're afraid to deal with the answer? Why are you interested in making drastic changes so abruptly?

2. **Talk it Out** - Get someone unbiased who can listen to you to talk it out without interjecting. In my experience, breakthroughs have happened when I've just rambled to my business coach or therapist because my guard has been let down. Find someone who you can talk at about what's going on and your reasoning behind making changes to see if you can work out the truth of the matter. And hey, maybe it really IS just that you need to scorch earth things and start from

scratch! At least talking it out will help you understand the "why" behind your decisions.

3. **Give it Some Space** - Large changes in business need time to gel, and you'll need to establish a plan for the inevitable hiccups that show up along the way, so try to give yourself a wide berth to set up a plan before putting things in motion or for getting your groove back.

4. **Decide if It's Really Worth Scrapping or If There's Something There** - This goes for both SOS and products/services you're thinking about discontinuing. When you feel that things are beyond repair and that big changes have to be made, try to figure out what good can come of it and strip it for parts. Your evergreen class about photography might not have been a big seller, but maybe it can get turned into a YouTube series that increases your social platform and gets you more business. In my own business I've:

    a. Used my old soap and skincare formulas and turned them into a book.

    b. Taken the knowledge I've learned as a Top Etsy Seller for vintage items and turned that into a book (you probably see a pattern here).

    c. Used a slide deck from my speaking gigs and turned it into an evergreen webinar series.

Staying the course and avoiding SOS can help you solidify your foothold in your marketplace, so it pays (literally) to do the hard work and figure a way through rather than bombing the whole project and starting from scratch, so reference this chapter whenever you're feeling a bit fidgety and wanting a big change.

CHAPTER 11: BAD DAYS AND BURN OUTS

Here's the worst day of my business life:

In late 2014 I went to a networking event in Manhattan solely because the head of a beauty distribution service was speaking on a panel. I met a few people, used my free drink tickets, but kept my eyes on her. I was there for her and her alone.

Normally, at least back then, I was fairly timid and would've rather run away screaming than tried to pitch someone at a party. But I knew this was my shot; her company could open huge, gilded doors for my business, and it was in my best interest to ask for her help.

She was speaking to someone when I tapped her on the shoulder, butting my way in I guess (though to be fair the conversation sounded like it was ending), introduced myself, and gushed about her company. How wonderful it was and how I would really love to partner with her brand as a small business owner who blah blah blah.

She was incredibly gracious and gave me her card, which I think I waited for the appropriate "cool girl" amount of time before using it. I emailed her, gushing again and saying how amazing it would be to work with her. She passed me off to one of her procurement people, and we were on our way.

The procurement woman (PW) was also very lovely and

felt like she was willing to be a champion for me, but I also understood that this business had a lot of moving parts and would have to go through multiple approval levels. I'd have to submit samples for them to review. If they gave me the approval, I would have to commit to a minimum of 20,000 units delivered to their warehouse for free.

To be fair, these were sample-sized, but even tiny products take time and cost money. However, I knew this would be my opportunity to skyrocket my business, and since I was so terrible at trade shows, this would be where I'd put that budget instead.

I sent over a sample of the product, though the packaging was yet to be finished as it would require a custom card, and I didn't want to do it without their okay, but instead I sent over proofs of concept. I got a tentative "go for it" and set a commitment to have the 20,000 units delivered to their warehouse for a November 2015 release.

There are many more efficient ways I could've completed this, but I didn't think I could afford it; really, I think I was just afraid. I ended up making, filling, labeling, packing and shipping all 20k units myself. I used a little whiteboard stuck on the back of my studio door to keep track of how many I had left to go. It took me all summer.

Cut to September when I follow up with PW to see about the contract that I had yet to receive and to arrange to ship. That's when she tells me:

"We've decided to pass on the order."

I felt like I had been sucker-punched and was about to vomit. I was sitting in a 120sq ft studio that was full of nothing but these 20,000 samples. I had no room to make anything else and had spent so much time devoted to this, and now it was gone. My god, what would I tell people when they asked?

What would I do? How would I get rid of all of these?

There's no way it would take me years of including them as gifts in orders and forget trying to unload them to multiple smaller distributors. They'd tell me to bring them something different and unique.

I had no contract. That just kept repeating in my head. "This was my fault, I took them at their word but never got it in official terms. How could you be so naive? You know better!" I wanted to scream, cry, run away, cry some more, and everything in between.

That was the worst day of my business life. Nothing has come close.

Know what happened?

I put on my "oh hell no" face and went back to the owner of the company. I forwarded her the original email that I had used as assurance this would be happening and asked her to please help because "it would look SUPER bad if anyone found out that your team ruined a small business and it really seems that you're not that kind of person, so I'm begging for your help."

Was it mildly threatening? Yeah, I guess so...but I was backed into a corner completely desperate and had to swing for the fences to give this one last shot. I sent the email and decided I had to get out of my studio for the rest of the day. I went to another friend's studio with my laptop and tried to focus on something, anything else.

PW emailed me the next day, saying she heard I spoke with the owner, and they *certainly* wouldn't want to do anything to hurt small business, so they're going to go ahead with the fulfillment. She was cheerful enough with the rest of the time we spoke, though I always felt a little sheepish like I got caught snitching.

That product ended up being one of the best-rated products on its website the month it launched. I got multiple paid reorders of full-sized products from them after.

Isn't that a crazy story? Truth be told, (and I swear on my dog this to be true) it's one I actually forgot about. I was listening to someone talk about a terrible day they had when something they said shot this memory right back into my brain. I can remember the facts and the outcome, but I can't remember the feeling of nausea. I don't feel the panic when I think about it, though I remember having a ton of it. I can remember reading and re-reading "We've decided to pass on this," trying to make my brain comprehend it, but I don't remember what the rest of the email said.

Bad Business Days Happen to Everyone

My point is, and I wish I could protect you from this like a little Business Mama Bear, but you are going to have traumatic days in business. You just are. My beautiful Business Baby Cub, I wish it weren't the case, but just as in life, business comes with breathtaking highs and unspeakable lows.

But it will pass. I promise you it will if you are willing to ride it out. Do what you have to do to get through it, there's no judgment here, but I will judge the crap out of you if you let it end your dream.

You know that quote that's about how you being yourself will piss people off, and that's a good thing? I think it was by Winston Churchill (or if not, it sounded Churchillian). That's true with running your own shop, too. There's going to be absolutely horrible customers, deals that fall through, materials that don't get delivered in time, tornados at your craft show, credit card bills that take your breath away. There are days when you'll wonder what the point of this all was and why you even bothered.

And look, I know you're expecting me to say, "but the highs just balance it out!" And sure, sometimes they do. But how many compliments do you remember? Now how many passive-aggressive statements or negative comments do you remember? More of the latter, right? Isn't it weird how our brain works when it comes to good stuff/bad stuff? Our brains are jerks.

On bad days, you can remind yourself of the good times. I like to keep my aforementioned little Jar of Awesome in my office full of folded-up post-it notes celebrating my wins. Truthfully though, I don't get around to unfolding those post-its as much as I could.

I'm one of those people who doesn't want to be reminded about the good stuff on a bad day, so I'm going to give you advice from that perspective. When a bad day shows up, and it's really a doozy, give yourself permission to let it go.

I usually do this by taking a walk, going to the gym to get my pump on while listening to angry music, whining to my husband and getting a hug, petting the dog, hugging my cats while they look confused and annoyed, or if it's really bad I take a Lorazepam, get my migraine hat out of the freezer, and go to bed. I let myself have a little pity party, and then I move on.

The moving on part is key. In my head, I've got too much stuff to do to dwell on that crappy moment, and I bet you're in the same boat. So I do my weird self-care pity party, then move onto another task. Once I get going on something else, I gain some perspective and start to detach myself from the situation. Would that be something your therapist recommends? Maybe, maybe not. In any case, it's worked for me for over a decade of business rollercoasters.

When Bad Days Become More Than a Little Bit of a Bummer

But what about when it doesn't? What about when things begin to weigh on you and don't go away?

One day (sometime after that whole 20k sample catastrophe), I was in the kitchen with Steve in our apartment back in Brooklyn, just lamenting over how my day went. Steve was listening and commiserating as he is so good at doing, then said to me, "You know, it doesn't sound like you're happy."

I was floored. One, because I was just talking about my normal day stuff. Two, because, wait a minute, *was I happy*? This person who was sharing my life and knew me better than anyone had just blindsided me. I had to think about what I was feeling. If he was wrong and I *was* happy with my choices, then I had to figure out why I was projecting something completely different.

Steve's comment rang in my ears for weeks. "It doesn't sound like you're happy." On the subway, on the walk to and from my studio, when I was making soap. "It doesn't sound like you're happy." My God, what have I done to my life?

He was right, and I wasn't happy. My business, the one I had grown since college, was not the dream I loved, but the job I hated. How could I fix it? If I gave it up, what else could I do? I didn't feel like I was good at anything else. Who would give me a job when I had no transferable skills?

I had begun to let the facade crack as it started to enter into my mind that I wanted out. I had officially burned out, and it wasn't salvageable. The escape hatch was now in view, and I was done putting out the fires in the spaceship (where am I even going with this analogy?)

I thought about selling the company; I had a lot of formulas that were really good products and had a loyal customer base, but honestly, I didn't want to deal with that. I spoke with a few business brokers, and it was an exhaustible mess to get everything into something that would be attractive to a buyer, especially when I hated it so much.

In the end, I just didn't want to go through all of the time, energy, questions, and insulting offers. Though I'd make more money selling than closing, I'd rather skip out on pretending I had anything left to give to the business while waiting for it to be sold. I just decided that for my mental health, it was necessary to rip off the band-aid, close the business, and walk away.

When I decided it was time to be done, I had SUCH elation. There was a lightness in me, in the way I moved, and the way I felt. What would I do for money? I wasn't entirely sure, but I knew enough avenues online that I could pick up some writing gigs, and maybe I could do that for a while. Maybe I could really devote time to my blog, Handmade Brooklyn (now MeganBrame.com), except make it more of a resource for entrepreneurs based on what I learned. Maybe I could run a podcast or a YouTube channel that helps other business owners.

I remember talking to friends I had made in my studio building, telling them I was closing down. They looked so concerned for me until I said, "no, this is what I want to do, and I'm really excited by it!"

I don't remember the specific feelings of my Super Bad Day of Business, but I do remember the feeling of walking out of my studio for the last time. It was empty except for a few stainless steel tables I had left for the next renter. I felt like I was supposed to give it one final, long look, so I did, but I didn't feel anything but impatience. I wanted to go!

I could've done cartwheels the whole way to the subway, I swear. It was a really lovely day.

Now, I guess this should go without saying, but I am not one to advocate digging in and staying the course if it's truly making you feel miserable. There's a difference between hustling through the hard times and killing yourself to avoid the hit to your pride that walking away can feel like.

Sometimes it's really hard to see the whole picture. I was

lucky that my husband decided it was time to say that to me, and I hope that you can have someone who intervenes when you can't see clearly.

Can you get your groove back after a burnout? Absolutely. Do you have to? Absolutely not. You get one life, live it in the best way you can.

If you're not ready to give in and you want to burn the burn out, here are some tips:

1. **Step back, even just for a day.** Take your physical body out of the space your business resides in and removes yourself from anything remotely resembling email or social media.

2. **Get to the root of your burn out.** What is it that's causing you to feel this way? Are you overworking yourself? Is it money? Journal, yes, actually get a notebook and do some free form writing about what it is that's blocking you from being happy.

3. **Take corrective action.** The only way to get through and keep going is if you're willing to make serious changes. Most likely, you're going to have to throw time or money at this. Start outsourcing menial work, or invest in apps that help take some of the workloads. Hire a business coach, go to therapy, pick up some freelance work to earn extra money. The keyword here is "action." You can't think your way out of a burnout; you have to correct your course and move your trajectory in a different direction.

This chapter is all about the neggy vibes, I know, and I apologize if it brings you down as that's in no way my intention. Also, can you imagine the book reviews on Amazon? "Bummed me out and made me never want to do anything. 2 stars."

Rather, I want you to take away some hope from this chapter. There will be bad days and times when you feel like giving up. You are human and completely awesome. I don't know you personally, but I do know that you've picked up this book because you're a driven person who is ready to take what she wants, and you want to be prepared as best you can. So read this chapter and understand that when you have a bad time, you'll get through it. You aren't alone, you aren't the first, and you can overcome any crappy thing that gets thrown your way.

Namaste.

CHAPTER 12: THE DEATH CARD

One thing I love about working with entrepreneurs in this day and age (Jesus, how old do I sound right now?) is that many of them are embracing their failures.

Wait, scratch that. Many of them recognize that they should embrace their failures, but all too often, then end up avoiding the uncomfortable lessons they would've learned.

Failure sucks, I get it. I've been over $30k in debt due to immature/impulsive business decisions, I've left expensive trade shows with 0 sales, and I've had to get day jobs to keep myself afloat. Failure is a hard pill to swallow, especially in a world where we're taught "just a little bit more; just a little bit further!" Sometimes, the better decision is to call it a day instead of letting an ego keep ahold of the reins.

But you know what? Failure, in the long run, isn't the worst thing to have to happen. The trade shows where I picked up 0 wholesale accounts? I received 3 of my 5 awards through them, The debt due to impulsive FOMO business opportunities? I paid it off eventually. The day jobs? They showed me that I not only know my stuff when it comes to marketing but that I have found my niche in the world and can command a premium price for it.

Now I'm going to tell you something you don't want to hear: You're going to mess up. You're going to have days where you wonder if you haven't made some terrible mistake. You're going to screw up an order that you'll have to refund or have a nasty customer who forgets that you're a person and not a faceless machine, or your website will go down right before launch.

I wish it weren't the case, but messing up is just par for the course when you're running your own business. The beauty of these failures, though, is the opportunity they provide you. I know that sounds a little cornball, but my own career as an entrepreneur and marketer has shown this to be true, so I can't pretend otherwise. Can you imagine if I was still making soap and candles? I'd never have written this book, gotten the chance to work with my coaching clients, or created any of the things I have today! Sure, I'd smell good, but my life would've been completely different.

This chapter is probably a "re-read" for you once you're out in the world running your business, so let me bypass the froo-froo happy feelings for you (because I imagine that if you are re-reading this chapter, today might've not been that great) and give you some actionable steps to get past failure.

How to Move Past a Serious Failure

1. **Take some time** - Don't respond to email, don't take phone calls about the situation, don't look at anything remotely related to your business. Get out of the space and have some self-care because you really deserve it. Bad things in life don't mean that you are bad, so let yourself have some distance from the situation.

2. **Figure out the lesson** - This has to come after taking some time, and it might not be a fast fix, but I guarantee that there is a way to learn from this crappy thing and to prevent it from happening again. When you're able to really get perspective on it, thank the Universe for the opportunity you were given with this and how better you are now because of it.

3. Take steps to prevent it from happening again

By the way, those bad things I mentioned earlier? They all happened to me. You know how I handled them?

1. Messed up an order and had to refund - Learned that I needed better packaging materials. Revamped my shipping process and insured anything that was more than $50 (as an aside here: I've found that the USPS is unequivocally the easiest shipping company to deal with when it comes to insurance claims. Just a little fun fact for you if you're planning a physical product-based business)

2. The mean customer who thought I was Walmart and not a person - Took my Lorazepam (anti-anxiety meds), hired a customer service rep to handle all correspondence and made videos of every possible scenario I could think of for her to refer to so I wouldn't ever have to see those emails again.

3. Website down before a launch - Sucked it up and paid more for the better hosting company. My site was back up within a few hours. Probably lost some sales, but I learned that hosting services are not something to cheap out on.

I named this chapter "The Death Card" because of a well-known trope with Tarot cards. If you're not familiar: there's a card in the deck that is just a picture of Death, usually depicted as the Grim Reaper or thereabouts. It sounds like a terrible card to get, right? Probably not something you want to see when you're asking the Tarot cards to let you know about your future.

The thing is, though, that Death is actually a very good card to see in a spread. Death doesn't mean your life or body is dying, but that something which has not been serving you is being changed out for something different. Will it be better? It's up to how you approach the new thing: if you take what you've learned with you, the change will prove to be a pivot point that may be crucial to your success. If you wallow in the loss, you'll never move past it.

"When God closes a door, He opens a window," isn't that how it goes? It's up to you to take advantage of every opportunity to grow as you start and grow your business. Failure is not the end and is not a death knell, especially if you take something from it.

One last thing: I think that entrepreneurs are afraid of failure because of the stigma that used to be attached to it. I say "used to" because I've found that most entrepreneurs I've met have worn their failures like badges of honor. I can't tell you how many times I've been at events or after parties (of conferences. I'm not cool enough for anything after 11 pm) where other entrepreneurs will sit around and tell their failures like funny "bad date" stories. All those people on Instagram who are ~living their best life~ have failed, probably in a spectacular fashion.

I know it because they wouldn't be there still, now, if they hadn't. They'd be abandoned accounts, with only one final "#blessed" comment. If you do not see their failures, that doesn't mean they haven't happened, and it's just that they're not ready to talk about it (or are still going through it). So instead of feeling inadequate because of Influencers, look at them through a different lens, between the travel posts and the beautiful clothes, to see the stumbles and the fallible person behind the pics.

CHAPTER 13: WHAT TO DO NEXT

In some way, it's oddly poetic that this is the last chapter you read because it's the last chapter I wrote for the book.

I've been staring at the title of this chapter in my Google Drive, avoiding diving into writing it because I honestly didn't know what to say. What to do next? Hell if I know!

But that's not true because you and I **do** know what you do next. We know because we've covered it in previous chapters! Let's rehash it together, shall we?

What you're going to do next:

- You're going to set up a plan for your business as best as you can
- You're going to do the hard homework and define your avatar, understand your SWOT analysis, and learn about the pros and cons of your industry.
-
- You're going to research and find the best legal structure for your business as you see fit.
- You're going to suck it up and hire people smarter than you to take some of the heavy liftings to set yourself up for success.
- You're going to set up your support network that includes family, friends, and competitors.
- You're going to acknowledge that you're not infallible

and that rough times may come, but you'll pull through them because you understand the need to be flexible.

- You're going to start small with a V1 product and get feedback to make it better and release subsequent versions and new products as you go.
- You're going to keep your eyes on your own paper and not compare someone else's Day 44,565 to your Day 1.
- You're going to do your own thing and not live someone else's dream.
- You're going to do this.

Now is the time to push you out of the nest so that you can open your wings and fly on your own. But don't worry, I'm still around to help you out. Let me know how your journey is going because I'd love to hear all about it!

Visit my blog for even more tips and to take the next step in your business adventure with my collection of tools, books, and courses, or reach out to work one on one with me through my High-Performance Marketing Coaching program. They're all available at www.meganbrame.com

This is your time, and you're ready to do it, so get to it.

Welcome to your Day 1.

LOVE AND THANKS

This book would still be clogging up my brain instead of these pages were it not for these amazing people:

First and foremost, thanks goes to my amazing ride-or-die husband, Steven Finkelstein, whose support through the good times and the bad have been crucial to getting me to where I am now. I am better in every way because of you. Also, you give the best hugs.

Special thanks and belly rubs to our pet kids: Bettie, Jeter, and Jimmy Bagels. Jimmy is staring and wagging his tail expectantly at me right now while I type this, so I better keep the rest of this short before I get a tennis ball shoved in my lap.

Thank you to Jarred Andrews, Jackie Damp, Laura Fisk, and Rachel Winard for being my sounding boards, guinea pigs, partners in crime, impromptu drinking buddies, and BFFs (both business and not).

Thank you to the professionals who keep me going and have heard about this book ad nauseam: Dr. Brian Amos, PhD, Dr. Matthew Fleig, MD, Joan Brenner, and Liz Wolfe. Speaking of professionals, thank you to those who came before me and taught me more than I could ever dream of learning, especially Pat Flynn, Amy Porterfield, Chalene Johnson, Rachel Hollis, Gary Vaynerchuk, and Tim Ferriss.

Thank you to those who helped me cut my marketing chops, especially including those who gave me a paycheck while doing so. Though we no longer work together in a corporate setting, I am eternally grateful for those who believed in my vision and trusted me with the marketing of their companies.

And lastly, but never least, thank you so so much to my readers, listeners, commenters, and anyone who has been able to decipher the streams of consciousness that are my blog posts and podcast episodes. This book would not happen without your help, your questions, and, most importantly, your support.

SWOT matrix courtesy of Depositphotos
Authors photo by Justin Hackworth

ABOUT THE AUTHOR

A 5x award-winning entrepreneur, blogger, coffee junkie, and marketing coach, Megan Brame has lived the ride as a small business owner for over a decade.

Her work has been featured in over a hundred publications, including the New York Times, OK! Magazine, Good Housekeeping, and the Huffington Post.

She currently resides in Upstate New York and teaches others how to develop their businesses from kitchen table side-hustles into full-time entrepreneur dreams on her blog meganbrame.com

What **if you could cr**eate the business you've al**ways** **wanted? A business th**at brings you success, gives **you the** income **that lets you** support your family, and op**ens up** the life you're ready to have?

Sounds great, right? The problem is, you have no **idea how** to do it.

Day 1 is made for you! In it, Megan covers the ste**ps you'll** take to make your dream a reality and launch **your suc**cessful business. Day 1 includes actionable tips **and sto**ries from Megan's own life as an award-winning **entrepre**neur who learned (sometimes the hard way) wha**t it takes** to make a successful business come to life.

Megan Brame is 5x award-winning entrepr**eneur,** author, podcaster, and **Marketing** Coach who has helped o**ther small** business owners achieve **success** through value-based m**arketing** initiatives. She current**ly resides** in Rochester, NY with **her** husband, two cats, dog, **and be**loved coffee maker. You **can find** her work, including the **podcast** "Stop Sucking at Business" **at** MeganBrame.com

www.ingramcontent.com/pod-product-compliance
Lightning Source LLC
Chambersburg PA
CBHW020550220526
45463CB00006B/2247